INTELLECTUAL PROPERTY RIGHTS

NIPA® GENX ELECTRONIC RESOURCES & SOLUTIONS P. LTD.
New Delhi-110 034

INTELLECTUAL PROPERTY RIGHTS

DRAFTING, INTERPRETATION OF PATENT SPECIFICATION AND CLAIMS

N.S. Rathore
Dean
College of Technology and Engineering
Maharana Pratap University of Agriculture and Technology
Udaipur, Rajasthan

S.M. Mathur
Associate Professor
College of Technology and Engineering
Maharana Pratap University of Agriculture and Technology
Udaipur, Rajasthan

Priti Mathur
College of Home Science
Maharana Pratap University of Agriculture and Technology
Udaipur, Rajasthan

Anshul Rathi
College of Technology and Engineering
Udaipur Rajasthan

NIPA® GENX ELECTRONIC RESOURCES & SOLUTIONS P. LTD.
New Delhi-110 034

NIPA® GENX ELECTRONIC
RESOURCES & SOLUTIONS P. LTD.

101,103, Vikas Surya Plaza, CU Block
L.S.C. Market, Pitam Pura, New Delhi-110 034
Ph : +91 11 27341616, 27341717, 27341718
E-mail: newindiapublishingagency@gmail.com
Web: www.nipabooks.com

For customer assistance, please contact
Phone: + 91-11-27 34 17 17
Fax: + 91-11- 27 34 16 16
E-Mail: feedbacks@nipabooks.com

ISBN: 978-8119215-55-3

Composed and Designed by NIPA®.

About the Editors

N.S.Rathore
Dean, College of Technology and Engineering, Udaipur
Rajasthan

N.S.Rathore has pursued M.Tech from Indian Institute of Technology, Delhi and Ph.D.RAU, Bikaner with specialization in Energy Studies. He is presently Dean of College of Technology and Engineering, Udaipur. He has a vast experience of 30 years in the university and engineering college in different capacities. He has been awarded 12 national and international awards including World Bank IDM-2007, Rajasthan Energy Conservation Award-2009 and Life time achievement award for activities of solar energy. He has authored 190 research papers in National and International Journals and published 32 books, 33 training manuals on various aspects of Agriculture Engineering, Renewable Energy, Environment Studies and Dairy & Food Technology. There are total 81 reports, proceeding, and 13 prototype developments, 71 popular articles of renewable Energy and Rural Development activities to his credit. He is member of number of professional & academic societies.

S.M.Mathur
Professor Department of Farm Machinery and Power Engineering, College of Technology and Engineering, Udaipur Rajasthan

Shailendra Mohan Mathur obtained his B.Tech. (Agril. Engg.) In 1984 from College of Technology and Agricultural Engineering (CTAE), Udaipur, M.Tech in Farm Machinery and Power Engineering in 1991 from IIT, Kharagpur, and Ph.D from CTAE, Udaipur in 2000. Presently he is working as Professor in the Department of Farm Machinery and Power Engineering, CTAE, Udaipur, Dr. Mathur has attended number of National and International conferences in India and abroad and delivered number of keynote presentations. He has a vast experience of 28 years in teaching, research and extension. He has published several papers in reputed international and national journals. Dr. Mathur has also edited 3 books and developed many folders. Dr. Mathur has guided several Masters and Ph.D. students. He has been awarded the FAO fellowship and visited USA and Thailand. He has also been the recipient of Arya Bhatt Samman, Life Time Education Achievement award and distinguished Service certificate from various organizations.

Dr. Priti Mathur

Research associate, college of Home Science, Udaipur Rajasthan

Dr. Priti Mathur, did her Master's Degree with specialization in Foods & Nutrition from Bombay University and Ph.D from Maharana Pratap University of Agricultural and Technology, Udaipur. She has an experience of more than 17 years in research & teaching and has taught UG classes in Sophia Girls College, Ajmer and is presently working as Research Associate in the Department of Planning and Monitoring, MPUAT, Udaipur. During her career she has actively participated and presented papers at national and international conferences, workshops and seminars and also has to hers credit papers published in national and international journals.

Mr. Anshul Rathi

Faculty in Management, College of Technology and Engineering, Udaipur, Rajasthan

Mr. Anshul Rathi holds a Master's Degree with specialization in Finance having an experience of more than 3 years in teaching and has taught UG and PG classes in B.N.P.G College, Pacific Institute of Management and is presently working as guest faculty in the Department of Master of Business Administration on contract basis in College of Technology and Engineering, Udaipur. During his career he has actively participated in TePP and TREMAP projects sponsored by Govt. of India. He has also actively participated and presented papers at national and international conferences, workshops and seminars and also has to his credit paper published in international journal.

Phone : 91-294-2471101 (O), 2427691 (R), Fax : 2470682
Email : vc_mpuat@yahoo.co.in

Maharana Pratap University of Agriculture and Technology
University Campus, Udaipur – 313 001 (Raj.) INDIA
महाराणा प्रताप कृषि एवं प्रौद्योगिकी विश्वविद्यालय
विश्वविद्यालय परिसर, उदयपुर – 313 001 (राज.)

डॉ. ओ. पी. गिल
कुलपति
Dr. O. P. Gill
Vice-Chancellor

No. P.S.: V.C.MPUAT: 2013: 1114 of 9.5.13

Foreword

Intellectual Property Right (IPR) is a tool for innovation and reward for value-adding creations of the human intellect that result from human ingenuity, creativity and inventiveness, Patenting and other forms of idea protection and largely considered to be a painful exercise with little or no benefit by innovators. Lack of understanding of the legal process and its economic benefits is a major roadblock. IPR plays a vital role in enhancing the socio-economic prosperity of the country. The economic functioning of IPR can be thought of as minimization of transaction costs and the optimization of time to fruition and avoidance of duplicate. Further, IPR provide incentives to invest on innovation, which in turn maximizes wealth of a nation. Hence, it enhances motivation to disseminate scientific and technological information which in turn stimulates R & D for improvement of the quality of life. There is a need to create large public awareness about the pivotal role of IPR in globalized knowledge economy. Keeping in view the significance of IPR to the society as a whole, College of Technology and Engineering, Udaipur had organized a two days' Workshop on **"Intellectual Property Right: Drafting, Interpretation of Patent Specification and claims'** Which was held during March 16-17, 2012 at College of Technology and Engineering, Udaipur (Rajasthan). The aim of workshop was to improve first hand exposure of current IP practices in India and associated aspects of prior art search, documentation, establishing patentability, attending office actions, claims drafting and interpretation etc.

A Patent document requires a combination of legal consideration and associated technical knowledge. The patent writing requires a very different writing style and articulation of associated technical and legal aspects. It is very difficult for an innovator or a scientist to hire a patent attorney to file his patent document because of high cost involvement and security reasons. It was felt that there is a need to have a book, which contains the papers of basics and fundamentals of IPR in India for innovators, teachers, scientists and innovative students to know the procedure of patent filling. I am happy that Dr. N S Rathore, Dr. S.M.Mathur, Dr. Priti Mathur and Mr. Anshul Rathi have made sincere effort to compile all useful information in this book.

This book entitled, **"Intellectual Property Rights: Drafting Interpretation of Patent Specification and Claims"** will be a useful reference document to individuals, entrepreneurs, innovators and university teachers who often are not fully aware as when and how to begin the task of protecting their research and innovation. The chapters included in this book will cover all aspects of patenting and its protection. The various case studies and pictorial illustrations make this book more informative and interesting. The brevity of the chapters, examples and exercises will make it interesting to all readers.

I would like to complement the editors and publishers for bringing out this excellent publication.

9thMay, 2013 **O.P.Gill**

Preface

In present situations the time for acquiring knowledge has become an important line for evaluating the success of university, institution, inventor, enterprise, government and industry; the shorter the time for gaining knowledge better will be the chances of success. Intellectual property rights (IPR) have become important in the face of changing technological environment, which is characterized by global competition, high innovation risks, short product cycle, need for rapid changes in technology, high investments in research and development (R & D) production & marketing and need for highly skilled human resources. In present geographical barriers to trade among nations are collapsing due to ICT intervention. Many products and technologies are simultaneously marketed and utilized in different countries. With the opening up of trade in goods and services intellectual property rights have become more susceptible to infringement leading to inadequate return to the creators of technology. In order to overcome this problem one has to file a patent application as early as possible before making it to public by any means.

Patent is monopoly right which is granted by the Government to the applicant for the full disclosure of an 'invention' which is 'new', inventive' and 'industrially applicable'. A patent application requires a combination of legal documentation and technical papers. This issue makes patent writing a very different writing style. The proper drafting of a patent application takes into account technical breadth, economic feasibility, legal strategy, conformance with a vast number of rules and regulations including socio-techno-economic feasibility. A well-defined patent application decides the fate of an invention. Drafting plays an important role in the success of any invention during its prosecution, management and maintenance during its tenure and turning into profit. Drafting a patent application is one of the most important and at the same time one of the difficult legal and technical process.

This book intellectual Property Rights: Drafting, Interpretation of Patent Specification and Claims is the compilation of the selected and invited papers out of those presented in the National Seminar on Intellectual Property Rights

Drafting, Interpretation of patent Specification and Claims, which was held during March 16017, 2012 at College of technology and Engineering, Udaipur (Rajasthan). This was attended by officials from the patent office, representatives of patent attorneys, innovators, scientists and incubation managers of various organizations. This book guides the drafting of patent applications from a practical perspective and gives all knowhow required to write a patent. Intended as an introductory text, it covers the entire process of drafting of a patent application and includes many helpful examples or case studies, illustrating the process from start to finish. Further, this to patentee on how to keep his patent alive. Looking to the increasing awareness among the inventors, investors and scientist and the increasing cost of patent attorneys, editors tried to publish a book containing papers from patent attorneys, scientist and innovators with practical case studies. This book will be helpful for invents, scientists, novice patent attorneys, agents, law students, and for those preparing for the patent bar exam.

We express our deep sense of gratitude to distinguished contributors of this book for their generosity in acceding to our request to share their valuable expertise. Prompt responses and encouragement received form them are gratefully acknowledge. We express our gratitude to Department of Scientific and Industrial Research, New Delhi, for their financial support for the Seminar and subsequent publication of this book.

Editors

Udaipur
May, 2013

Contributors

Mr. Anshul Rathi
Assistant Professor
College of Technology and Engineering
Udaipur, Rajasthan

Mr Anil Pandey
IPR Consultant
Ahmedabad, Gujarat

Dr. D.R. Agarwal
Director
ITAG Business Solutions Ltd.
Kolkata, West Bengal

Dr. K.S. Kardam
Deputy Controller of Patents & Designs
and Head of Office
Patent Office, Delhi

Dr Manish Kumar
Associate Professor
Department of Production and Industrial Engineering
MBM Engineering College, JNV University
Jodhpur, Rajasthan

Dr. N.S. Rathore
Dean
College of Technology and Engineering
Udaipur, Rajasthan

Ms. Nidhi Bhatt
Patent Agent
H K Acharya & Company
Ahmedabad, Gujarat

Dr. Pradeep Srivastava
Associate Professor
School of Biochemical Engineering
Institute of Technology
Banaras Hindu University
Varanasi, Uttar Pradesh

Dr P.K. Ghosh
Professor & Head
Deptt. of Metallurgical and Materials Engineering,
IIT, Roorkee
Uttar Pradesh

Ms. Poornima Ganesh
IPR Consultant
B-209, Golden Residensy
Outer Ring Road Bellandur
Banglore-

Dr. Priti Mathur
Research Associate
College of Home Science
MPUAT, Udaipur
Rajasthan

Ms. Rajeshwari Hariharan
Partner
Rajeshwari & Associates
Delhi

Ms. Shalini Singh
Associate Professor
School of Biochemical Engineering
Institute of Technology
Banaras Hindu University
Varanasi, Uttar Pradesh

Dr. S.M. Mathur
Associate Professor, Department of FM&PE
College of Technology and Engineering
Udaipur
Rajasthan

Mr. S.K. Swarup
Assistant Controller (P&D)
Intellectual Property Office, Delhi
Ministry of Commerce and Industry
Government of India

Mr. Vimal Kumar Varun
Scientist 'F', Department of Scientific & Industrial Research
Technology Bhawan
New Mehrauli Road
New Delhi

Contents

1

Working of Patents in India

K.S. Kardam

Abstract

The two most important tasks for a patentee to undertake after being granted a patent, in any patent regime, would be to pay the renewal fees necessary to keep the patent alive, and provide proof of having worked the patent in the jurisdiction. This article seeks to highlight features of India's legal requirements with regard to the working of patents on a commercial scale. The number of patents granted in a country is an indicator of the technological strength of the country. However, it should be noted that actual technological growth depends upon the working of patents. Working of a patent means the commercial exploitation of the invention that is embodied in the patent.

Keywords: Patents, Non-working, compulsory license, Importation

The Requirement that Patents be Worked

At the heart of aIndian Patent Act, lies the general principle that patents are granted '*not merely to enable patentees to enjoy a monopoly on a patented article*', but '*to secure that the inventions are worked in India on a commercial scale and to the fullest extent that is reasonably practicable without undue delay*'. An addendum is a requirement that '*the protection and enforcement of patent rights contribute to technological innovation, the transfer and dissemination of technology, to the mutual advantage of producers and users of technological knowledge, and in a manner conducive to social and economic welfare, and to a balance of rights and obligations*' [Section 83 of the Patents (Amendment) Act, 2005].The Act requires every patentee and every licensee (whether exclusive or otherwise) to provide information on the extent to which the 'patented invention' has been worked on a commercial scale in India .

Failure to supply such information is a punishable offence and invites a fine which may extend to rupees ten lakh. Additionally, knowingly furnishing false information is an offence punishable with imprisonment for up to six months, a fine or both [Sec. 122]. This penalty is also by no means insignificant, especially when one realizes that it was increased by a multiple of 50 from its previous level. Clearly, it indicates that such an offence is considered to be a grave offence to impose such a hefty fine.

The relevant information is to be submitted by patentees and licensees in a Statement Regarding the Working of the Patented Invention, as per Form 27, provided in the Second Schedule to the Patent (Amendment) Rules, 2006. This information includes the following:

1. Whether the invention has been worked;
2. If not worked, the reasons for not working the invention, and the steps being taken to work the invention;
3. If worked, quantum and value (in rupees) of the patented product:
    a. manufactured in India,
    b. imported from other countries, giving details of the countries concerned;
4. licenses and sub-licenses granted during the year;
5. Whether the public requirement has been met, at a reasonable price either partly, adequately or to the fullest extent.

The Patent Rules requires that this information should be filed every financial year, within three months of the end of each year. Thus, the latest that a patentee or licensee can file such information for a given calendar year is 31st March of the following year.

Working of Patents in India

As the patents are granted to encourage the inventions and also to secure that inventions are worked in India on a commercial scale to the fullest extent that is reasonably practicable time without undue delay. This cast a duty on the patentee to make efforts for commercial working of the patented invention at the earliest but not later than three years from the date of Grant of Patent.However, failure on the part of the patentee to ensure the commercial working of the patent within the said period would make , any interested person entitled to seek a Compulsory licence.

Availability of Information

The provisions in the Patents Act,empowers the Controller General to call for the information of working from the patentee or a licensee or otherwise, to furnish such information within two months from the date of notice sent for this purpose or within further time period as may be allowed by him. The Controller may publish the information received by himin such manner as may be prescribed in an official journal which is published periodically by Indian Patent Office.

Prior to the amendments in the Patent Act, in 2005 , the information relating to the Commercial Working of Patented Information, viz., the patent number, the date of patent, the name and address of the patentee and the title of the invention were used to be published in the Gazette of India. However, the Annual Reports published by the Controller General of Patents, Designs & Trademarks contains the information regarding the number of patents commercially worked during a particular year.

Non-working Patents, Compulsory Licensing and Revocation

At any time after three years of the grant of a patent, any person interested may apply to the Controller for a compulsory license on the patent on grounds that, inter alia, the patented invention is not worked in India. While considering such an application, the Controller shall take into account several factors, including the nature of the invention, the measures taken by the patentee/licensee to use the invention, and whether or not the applicant for a compulsory licence tried to obtain a voluntary licence from the patentee. According to the Manual of Patent Practice and Procedure (in para 18.2.6:4), a non-working invention will be assessed by reference to the facility available in India for working, or otherwise. It is, therefore, permissible to import the patented invention. However, "*mere importation without exploring the possibility of manufacturing in India*"could be a factor in assessing the status of the patented invention. [Controller Generals Decision in NATCO Vs. BAYERS (http://ipindia.nic.in/ipoNew/compulsory_License_12032012.pdf)]

Two years after the grant of the first compulsory licence, anyone may apply to the Controller to revoke the patent, if, inter alia, the patented invention has not been worked in India. The onus lies on the applicant to furnish the facts upon which such revocation is sought and the nature of the applicant's interest. Such an application must ordinarily be decided within one year of its presentation to the Controller.

Conclusion

While a great deal of importance for working of patent in India is placed in the Act, however, some of the individual patentee may not be aware of such issues due to lack of awareness of such statutory requirement under the Patent Act. Due to such lack of awareness and failure on their part to comply with the requirements under the law to provide such information, they could be liable for penal provisions without any intention to withhold such information. It is therefore suggested that information regarding commercial working of the patents should be provided to the Patent Office timely by the patentee to meet the obligations under the law to avoid implications of penal provisions. It is also suggested that more awareness is required from the Government, Scientific organisations to disseminate such provisions.

References

Annual Report, 2006-07, Intellectual Property Office, India, Available at: http://ipindia.gov.in/cgpdtm/AnnualReport_English_2006-2007.pdf

Manual of Patent Practice and Procedure, Intellectual Property Office, India, Available at: http://ipindia.nic.in/ipr/patent/DraftPatent_Manual_2008.pdf

The Patents Act, 1970, as amended by The Patents (Amendment) Act, 2006

The Patents Rules, 2003, as amended by The Patents (Amendment) Rules, 2006

http://ipindia.nic.in/ipoNew/compulsory_License_12032012.pdf (NATCO Vs. BAYER)

2

IPR and Innovation

Pradeep Srivastava and Shalini Singh

Introduction

'IP' refers to unique, value-adding creations of the human intellect that results from human ingenuity, creativity and inventiveness. An IP right is thus a legal right, which is based on the relevant national law encompassing that particular type of intellectual property right. Such a legal right comes into existence only when the requirements of the relevant IP law are met and, if required; it is granted or registered after following the prescribed procedure under that law. All countries around the world have a national legal system of intellectual property rights which has developed over varying periods of time during the last 150 years or so. It has enabled the grant of property-like rights over such new knowledge and creative expression of mankind, which has made it possible to harness the commercial value of the outputs of human inventiveness and creativity. This is usually done by its orderly use, exchange or sharing it amongst various types of business partners in a complex network of strategic relationships that generally work harmoniously during the new product development process for creating and marketing new and improved goods and services in domestic and export markets.

IPR is a tool for Innovation and reward for it. Innovations are concerned with the commercialization of new ideas; in contrast, an 'invention' may not be directly associated with commercialization. As such, innovation may be seen as a process of interaction and feedback during the various stages of the new product development process. An invention is considered as the generation of a new idea or knowledge, which aims to solve a specific technical problem. Inventions could relate to products or processes and are characteristically protected by trade secrets, utility models/petty patents or patents. Utility models/petty patents or patents are granted/registered under the relevant national/regional law by the relevant national or regional patent office. As not all inventions are commercialized, so it is clear that not all inventions result in innovations.

Knowledge

"Knowledge is information that changes something or somebody — either by becoming grounds for actions, or by making an individual (or an institution) capable of different or more effective action." — Peter F. Drucker in *The New Realities.*

Knowledge is a familiarity with someone or something, which can include facts, information, descriptions, or skills acquired through experience or education. It can refer to the theoretical or practical understanding of a subject. It can be implicit (as with practical skill or expertise) or explicit (as with the theoretical understanding of a subject); and it can be more or less formal or systematic. According to Dr. APJ Abdul Kalam Honorable President of India: *"Thinking provides knowledge, Knowledge makes you great."*

Knowledge establishes a paradox to its dimensions. It can be briefly defined as:-

- Using knowledge does not consume it but it does get obsolete
- Transferring knowledge does not lose it but market mechanisms allow ownership
- Knowledge is abundant, but the ability to use it is scarce
- Producing knowledge resists organisation.
- Much of it walks out the door at the end of the day

According to Achterbergh & Vriens (2002) "The role of knowledge in generating appropriate actions is that it serves as a background for articulating possible courses of action (articulation), for judging whether courses of action will yield the intended result and for using this judgment in selecting among them (selection), for deciding how actions should be implemented and for actually implementing actions (implementation)".

Knowledge Pyramid

Knowledge is develops like a pyramids. "Knowledge Pyramid", refers loosely to a class of models for representing purported structural and/or functional relationships between **d**ata, **i**nformation, **k**nowledge, and **w**isdom. "Typically information is defined in terms of data, knowledge in terms of information, and wisdom in terms of knowledge".

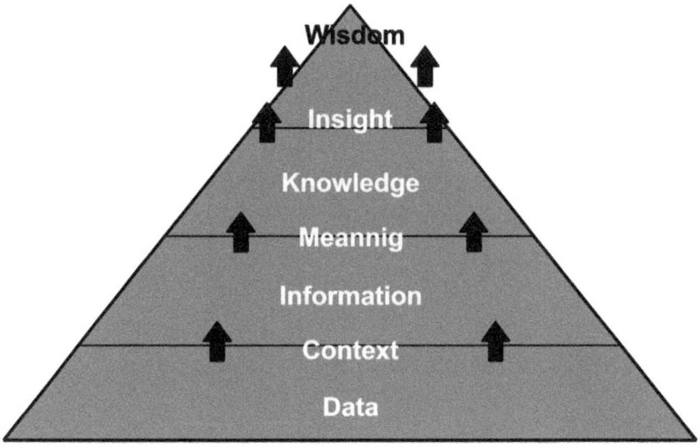

Fig. 1: Knowledge pyramid

Knowledge Management

Knowledge management (KM) comprises a range of strategies and practices used in an organization to identify, create, represent, distribute, and enable adoption of insights and experiences. Such insights and experiences comprise knowledge, either embodied in individuals or embedded in organizations as processes or practices. Different definition of knowledge managements (KM) are given below-

- A multi-disciplined approach to achieving organisational objectives by making the best use of knowledge.
- The systematic processes, by which knowledge needed for an organisation to succeed is created, captured, shared and leveraged.
- The art of creating commercial value from intangible assets.

Innovations

Innovation is the creation of better or more effective products, processes, services, technologies, or ideas that are accepted by markets, governments, and society. Innovation differs from invention in that innovation refers to the use of a new idea or method, whereas invention refers more directly to the creation of the idea or method itself.

Emphasizing the role of innovation, Jack Welch, MD of GE says that "I am convinced that if the rate of change inside the institution is less that the rate of change outside, the end is in sight. The only question is timing of the end".

To evaluate the correlation between innovation, creativity and intelligence it may be said

- That innovation is using an existing idea for a laterally different purpose or application.

- Whereas creativity is doing things that has not done before.
- And the intelligence is the ability to learn and think.

Innovation Process

An innovation starts as a concept that is refined and developed before application. Innovations may be inspired by reality. The innovation process, which leads to useful technology, requires:

- Research
- Development (up-scaling, testing)
- Production
- Marketing
- Use

The complete process of innovation is detailed in Fig.2. The hidden factor in the innovation process is the utility or demand of the discovery which, is finally governed by the market dynamics.

Research
↓
Discovery
↓
Development
↓
Patenting and approval
↓
Marketing
↓
Adaptation

Fig. 2: Figure showing the process of innovation

Drivers of Innovation

Various factors encourage an organization to innovate. Each of these drivers demands continuous innovation and learning so that the process can be repeated continuously. These drivers also help to create a sense of urgency around the need to create new organizational goals and generate new ideas for meeting these goals. These drivers can be summarized as follows:

- Emerging technologies
- Competitor actions
- New ideas from customers, strategic partners, and employees

- Emerging changes in the external environment

However the five myths of innovations are

- Innovation is about creating a hot new product... New products are swiftly copied and rarely enjoy sustained profits.
- Innovation comes from being creative... It is far likelier to come from being disciplined.
- Innovation is expensive, demanding lots of resources... Failure to innovate is what is costly.
- Create hundreds of ideas because of high failure rates... Fewer, bolder ideas based on your company's capabilities and unmet customer needs you discover work best.
- Early financial analysis is key to approving concepts... Nearly always wrong—build prototypes instead.

National Knowledge Commission

On 13 June 2005, the Prime Minister of India, Dr. Manmohan Singh, constituted the **National Knowledge Commission**, as a think-tank charged with considering possible policy that might sharpen India's comparative advantage in the knowledge-intensive service sectors. The NKC websites was launched in February 2006.

In particular, the Commission was to advise the Prime Minister's Office on policy related to education, research institutes and reforms needed to make India competitive in the knowledge economy. The Commission was to recommend reform of the education sector, research labs, and intellectual property legislation; as well as consider whether the Government could itself upgrade its use of the latest techniques to make its workings more transparent.

The Terms of Reference of the NKC are

- "Build excellence in the educational system to meet the knowledge challenges of the 21st century and increase India's competitive advantage in fields of knowledge.
- Promote creation of knowledge in Science and technology laboratories.
- Improve the management of institutions engaged in Intellectual Property Rights.
- Promote knowledge applications in Agriculture and Industry.
- Promote the use of knowledge capabilities in making government an effective, transparent and accountable service provider to the citizen and promote widespread sharing of knowledge to maximize public benefit."

Intellectual Property Rights (IPRs)

Intellectual property is unique, as it is the fruit of personal creation and inventiveness. It might be a poem that one writes, the name your hairdresser thinks up to sell his or her services, or a mother's invention for a non-spill cup for babies. It can also be a Picasso painting, an Akira Kurosawa film, a Naguib Mahfouz novel, a new method of irrigation for farmers in arid regions, the invention of the light bulb, a computer chip or a jet turbine engine.

An IP right provides the right holder with an exclusive right to stop others. By according to this right, society provides an incentive for people and organizations to invest time, resources and original thinking to develop innovative products and technologies and expand knowledge and culture. This encourages the production of a wide range of quality goods and services, and helps maintain fair competition.

In the future, intellectual property creators aim to deliver more abundant food resources, clean energy and cures for illnesses from cancer to the common cold. In virtually every instance, intellectual property stimulates progress, transforming society and adding value to our lives.

Almost everyone in society is a user and potential creator of intellectual property. Its protection, through a system of national and international rules called intellectual property rights, is necessary to provide incentives and financing for innovation and creation, which in turn lead to economic, cultural and social progress. Protection for intellectual property also encourages the production and dissemination of knowledge and a wide range of quality goods and services. Intellectual property rights add value for consumers and can provide a guarantee of source and quality.

Intellectual property protection contributes to economic growth in both developed and developing countries by stimulating innovation, cultural diversity and technical development as part of a larger policy framework. Properly used, intellectual property rights can also be key tools for the alleviation of poverty through trade.

Society provides legal rights over intellectual property to encourage the production of inventions and creative works that benefit society and to help innovators and creators make a living from their work. These rights, which can belong to individuals or organizations, are recognized by governments and courts. The system is designed to benefit society as a whole, in both developed and developing countries, striking a delicate balance to ensure that the needs of both the creator and the user are satisfied. This balance is maintained through checks within the intellectual property system itself and in the larger regulatory framework, to ensure that the system is sustainable and beneficial to all stakeholders.

Almost all businesses in all countries – the vast majority of which are small enterprises use trademarks for marketing their goods and services. Copyrights are even more easily available. The moment someone writes a text, composes some music or draws an image, he or she will have copyright to the result. Intellectual property law limits what can be protected and for how long. Intellectual property rights do not protect ideas. They protect only expressions of ideas, in the case of copyrights, and inventions fulfilling certain strict and well-established criteria in the case of patents. These limitations and conditions are built-in mechanisms to balance the rights of intellectual property owners with the interests of society. Intellectual property rights allow innovators and creators to choose the terms on which they distribute their work. They can choose, for example, to license and sell their works or inventions, to make them available for free, or to allow their use subject to certain conditions.1In the patent area, patented technologies are shared on certain terms as common technical standards to improve the interoperability of different systems, thus simplifying the lives of consumers. Looking forward, as economies develop, the use and value of intellectual capital will gradually replace the value of raw materials as a percentage of capital input toward economic growth. As such, intellectual property is an increasingly important asset that must be continually nurtured, protected and stimulated to grow.

Rationale behind IPRs

Some of the basic forms of IPR protection in today's society are-

- Patents

To stimulate innovation/encourage investment the inventor receives an exclusive right to his invention in exchange for disclosure of the invention in such a way that it allows replication; the inventor receives a limited amount of time to recoup his investment.

- **Trademarks**

Protection of goodwill and reputation.

- Copyright

Protection of creativity

- Design registration

Every country has its own Paten laws, but the most blatant explanation is that: Everything under the sun that is made by man. And Ideas/ invention are patentable. However some of the basic requirements of a patenting are

- New/ novelty
- Inventive step/non-obviousness (not obvious to someone skilled in the art)
- Industrial Applicability
- Patentable subject matter

The Exclusions from patentability as per law are the following:-

- Discoveries are not patentable: Einstein could not patent his celebrated law that $E = mc^2$; nor could Newton have patented the law of gravity. Such discoveries are "manifestations of . . . nature, free to all men and reserved exclusively to none"
- Literary, dramatic, musical or artistic works
- Schemes, rules, games, computer programs as such
- Methods of medical treatment
- Contrary to public policy and morality: Those which by publication or exploitation might result in offensive, immoral or anti-social behavior. Current debate life patents/GM Food
- Plant and animal varieties (in EU not in US)

TRIPS Agreement

The TRIPS Agreement, which came into effect on 1st January 1995, is to date the most comprehensive multilateral agreement on intellectual property. The areas of intellectual property that it covers are: copyright and related rights (i.e. the rights of performers, producers of sound recordings and broadcasting organizations); trademarks including service marks; geographical indications including appellations of origin; industrial designs; patents including the protection of new varieties of plants; the layout-designs of integrated circuits; and undisclosed information including trade secrets and test data.

The three main features of the TRIPS agreement are:

i. Standards

ii. Enforcement

iii. Dispute settlement

TRIPS have the following objectives will referred to IPR

- The promotion of technological innovation; The transfer &dissemination of technology; to the mutual advantage of producers and users of technological knowledge.
- IP protection is not an end in itself, but one means to promote public policy objectives.

However TRIPS define the minimum standard of IP protection. TRIPS provides for mandatory minimum standards of protection in most IP categories. In general, Members in domestic laws may not provide less protection than under TRIPS. Members may provide higher protection than under TRIPS. While the countries were debating on TRIPS agreement and public health, a forceful debate was declared on 14/11/2001. It declared that:-

- "we recognize the gravity of the public health problems afflicting many developing and least-developed countries, especially those resulting from HIV/AIDS, tuberculosis, malaria and other epidemics" (par 1)
- "we recognize that IP protection is important for the development of new medicines. We also recognize its effects on prices" (par 3)
- "we agree that the TRIPS does not and should not prevent members from taking measures to protect public health, TRIPS should be interpreted and implemented in a manner supportive of public health and promote access to medicines".

Compulsory Licensing

This amendment was a specific reference to pharmaceutical industry IPR and its further commercialization. Section 92A, which was inserted by the ordinance in pursuance of paragraph 6 of the Doha Declaration on TRIPS, has been further amended. Now, compulsory license to manufacture and export the patented product to any country having insufficient or no manufacturing capacity in the pharmaceutical sector can also be granted if such country has allowed importation of the patented pharmaceutical products from India. The amended provision will allow Indian companies to produce and export AIDS drugs to African and South East Asian countries.

The Amendment has greatly broadened the scope of opposition to the patent by introducing two changes; that is after its publication but before its grant and after the grant, within one year.

Indian Patent Act

Indian patent law tells the important aspects of Indian Patent Act, 1970. India patent Act, 1970 differentiates patentable and non-patentable inventions. It means distinction is made between invention and process of invention. Person should have been true inventor of the product in order to be eligible under Indian law. Person whom patent right has been granted is known as patentee. Patentee has monopoly right over creation, right to surrender, right to give patent to some other person. This right is given by a state in order to safeguard and protect his invention. Under Patent Act, right to prevent others from making any use, selling or distributing the invented patent without any permission from patentee. In case there is an infringement of the patentee's law then a suit may be filed for infringement.

Patent Right varies from country to country. In India the law which govern patent right is "Indian Patent Act 1970". Indian Patent Act, 1970 grants exclusive right to the inventor for his invention for limited period of time. Generally 20 years time has been granted to the patent holder but in case of inventions relating to manufacturing of food or drugs or medicine it is for seven years from the date of patent. There is certain legal procedure which needs to be followed in order to register. There are several attorney helping inventor in patent registration by providing them best well informed knowledge. In India patent registration can be filed individually or jointly. In case of deceased inventor this can be done his legal representative on behalf of him. All the required documents need to be filed along with the application form. Only after verification registration certificate is provided to the applicant.

Stages of Patent Filling

Although most inventors are concerned with the rights a patent grants during its monopoly, or in-force, period (from the date the patent issues until it expires), the law actually recognizes five "rights" periods in the life of an invention. These five periods are as follows:

1. **Invention conceived but not yet documented.** When an inventor conceives an invention, but hasn't yet made any written, signed, dated, and witnessed record of it, the inventor has no rights whatsoever.

2. **Invention documented but patent application not yet filed.** After making a proper, signed, dated, and witnessed documentation of an invention, the inventor has valuable rights against any inventor who later conceives the same invention and applies for a patent. The invention may also be treated as a "trade secret" — that is, kept confidential — which gives the inventor the legal right to sue and recover damages against anyone who immorally learns of the invention (for example, through industrial spying).

3. **Patent pending (patent application filed but not yet issued).** During the patent pending period, including the one-year period after a provisional patent application is filed, the inventor's rights are the same as in Period 2 above. With one exception, discussed below, a patent application does not give an inventor any extra rights — only the hope of a future monopoly that begins when a patent issues. However, most companies that manufacture a product that is the subject of a pending patent application will mark the product "patent pending" in order to warn potential copiers that if they copy the product, they may have to stop later (and thus scrap all their molds and tooling) if and when a patent issues.

   Eighteen months after filing, and while the application is pending, the U.S. Patent and Trademark Office (USPTO) will publish the application unless the applicant files a Non publication Request at the time of filing and doesn't file for a patent outside the U.S. If the application is published during the pendency period, an inventor can later obtain royalties from an infringer from the date of publication provided (1) the application later issues as a patent; and (2) the infringer had actual notice of the published application.

4. **In-force patent (patent issued but hasn't yet expired).** After the patent issues, the patent owner can bring and maintain a lawsuit for patent infringement against anyone who makes, uses, or sells the invention without permission. The patent's in-force period lasts from the date it issues until it expires. Also, after the patent issues, it becomes a public record or publication that blocks others from getting patents on the same or similar inventions — that is, it becomes "prior art" to anyone who files a subsequent patent application.

5. **Patent expired.** After the patent expires, the patent owner has no further rights, although infringement suits can still be brought for any infringement that occurred during the patent's in-force period, as long as the suit is filed within the time required by law. An expired patent remains a valid "prior-art reference" forever.

Why Controversial?

Create semi-monopolies also covering goods that might be essential to society (e.g. pharmaceuticals and environmentally sound technologies) /raises prices (higher than production costs)

- Limit access to textbooks, educational material, information
- Impacts on reverse engineering and imitation
- Exceptions are pushed to the limit/scope is widened:
- Extension of subject matter - - patentability of life / software;
- Extension of term of protection — 70 years of copyright protection;
- Creation of new rights — non original databases;
- over relaxation of granting of patents — lack of adequate description;
- inclusion of IP in trade, investment and stand alone agreements;
- primacy of private rights of public rights

IPR and Development

Most of the work reported above treats IPR as an exogenous policy choice, and then investigates its effect on economic behavior in the form of innovation, investment, and technology transfer. There is also a considerable literature that examines the political economy of IPR, looking at the economic determinants of IPR policy in the history of a country at different stages of economic development or a cross-section of countries at different level of economic development. At a low level of economic development, countries develop by bridging their technology gap through imitation. A weak IPR regime serves to reduce the cost of imitation. But as they develop indigenous innovation capability so that they start producing intellectual property, the welfare calculus changes such that countries find it in their own interest to strengthen IPR protection. This pattern of association between IPR and development has been affirmed in studies that investigate the historical relationship between the two, as well as those that use contemporary, cross-country data. The correlation between innovation performance and economic development has strengthened over the past 15 years. Technological progress is now responsible for up to one half of the growth of the US economy8 and, in 2000; intangible assets represented 70 percent of corporate assets in the United States. Creative industries, such as publishing, music, film, software and arts, are a powerful generator of economic growth and employment in both the developed and developing world. These industries –heavily reliant on copyright – contributed more than 1.2 trillion euros to the EU's economy, produced added value of 450 billion euros, equalling 5.3% of the EU's GDP, and employed 5.2 million persons in 2000.

Global Innovation Index (GII)

The Global Innovation Index is computed as an average of the scores across inputs pillars (describing the enabling environment for innovation) and output pillars (measuring actual achievements in innovation). Five pillars constitute the Innovation Input Sub-Index: 'Institutions,' 'Human capital and research,'

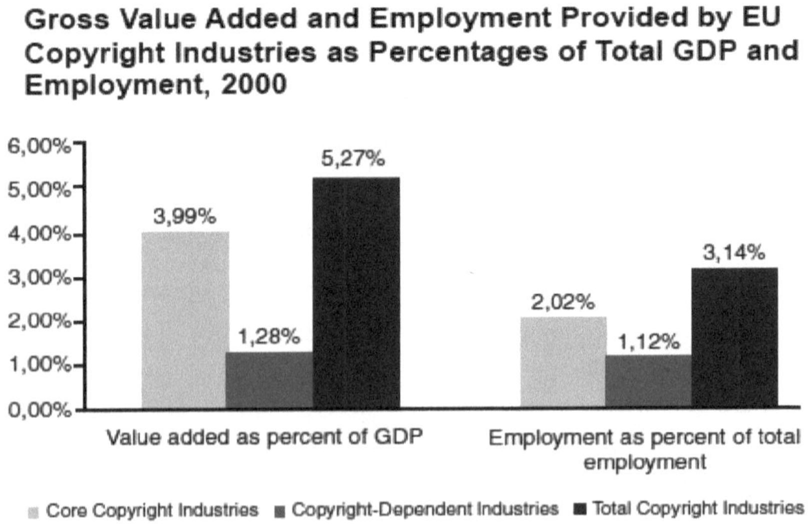

Fig.3: GDP and Employment

Source: Turku school of Economics and Business Administration, prepared for European Commission, Directorate General, Internal Market, The Contribution of copyright and Related Rights to the European Economy, 20 October, 2003.

'Infrastructure', 'Market sophistication' and 'Business sophistication'. The Innovation Output Sub-Index is composed of two pillars: 'Scientific outputs' and 'Creative outputs'. The Innovation Efficiency Index, calculated as the ratio of the two Sub-Indices, examines how economies leverage their enabling environments to stimulate innovation results. Global Innovation Index (GII), ranks countries on the basis of an enabling environment provided to industry and institutions for coming out with innovative practices. The key to move forward is increased level of funding for R&D in scientific, engineering, economics and business areas. India is the ninth most efficient country when it comes to innovation, according to a study conducted by the Confederation of Indian Industry (CII).

Glimpse of India and China

Patents issued by both China and India are their quality. Using patent citation ratios is an important measure to accessing patent quality. Tseng (2009) points out that patent quality is extremely heterogeneous in China and India, with a few patents of high quality with most being low quality, with the same average citation ratio of 3.6 for both countries.

The Indian and Chinese demand for patents through the PCT system has grown at annual rates in the range of 40-60%, while for the advanced economies the corresponding rates are in the range of 10-20% and for South Korea slightly above 30%. Understanding the no of PCT, for China and India, in the most recent decades has also been accompanied by high growth in the demand for patents, thus indicating that not only imitation has been part of that process but also that innovation capabilities have actively been fostered.

Remarkable technological specialization of both India and China, with a concentration of 61% and 37% respectively in their PCT filings in the top three classes (IT, Pharma, BT). China more concentrated in classes related to telecommunications and electronics, for India the most important classes of technological specialization are related to pharmaceuticals, fine chemistry and medical technology.

Conclusions

To make the intellectual property system work for their countries and communities, Governments must take positive action. Suggested measures include: providing for clear and enforceable intellectual property rights ownership, without discrimination as to nationality; improving the accessibility of national and international intellectual property systems by keeping the costs of obtaining, maintaining and enforcing intellectual property rights low; ensuring that procedures for obtaining, maintaining and enforcing intellectual property rights are simple and user-friendly; harmonizing intellectual property systems and cooperating internationally to simplify and reduce costs for obtaining rights in several countries thereby helping inventors and creators disseminate their innovations and creative products globally. ensuring that intellectual property institutions are efficient and sufficiently funded; supporting intellectual property policies with sound economic management, good infrastructure and other appropriate policies in areas such as education, science and technology, culture, taxes, investment regulations, production and technical incentives, trade, and competition; establishing an active and coherent intellectual property policy coordinated throughout government bodies; educating local communities, businesses and the public on the potential benefits of the intellectual property system; providing assistance to innovators/producers/creators on how to use intellectual property protection to their commercial advantage and supporting efforts of stakeholder organizations in this area; bridging the gap between academic and research institutions, and businesses and financing sources; and taking action against counterfeiting and piracy by making it a priority to strengthen and/or create a legal framework to ensure implementation and effective enforcement measures against intellectual property theft.

References

Greenhalgh, C. and Rogers M., (2010) Innovation, Intellectual Property, and Economic Growth. New Jersey: Princeton University Press.

Miller, Arthur Raphael, and Michael, H. (2000) Davis. Intellectual Property: Patents, Trademarks, and Copyright. 3rd ed. New York: West/Wadsworth.

The Agreement on Trade-Related Aspects of Intellectual Property Rights (TRIPS)

Roth, S. (2009) 'New for whom? Initial images from the social dimension of innovation', International Journal of Innovation and Sustainable Development **4**(4):231-252.

The Hindu: Tamil Nadu News: Vice-Chancellors constantly under political pressure, laments academic.

The Hindu : National : Knowledge panel clarifies suggestions.

Patent Rights in India, January 2008.

Rowley, Jennifer (2007) "The wisdom hierarchy: representations of the DIKW hierarchy". Journal of Information Science, **33**(2):163–180.

Zins, Chaim, (2007) "Conceptual Approaches for Defining Data, Information, and Knowledge" (PDF). Journal of the American Society for Information Science and Technology (Wiley Periodicals, Inc.) **58**(4):479–493.

The global innovation index 2011. Stuart Pallister, "Pushing the boundaries: innovation or imitation in China and India?"

3

Indian IP SWOT Regime and New Way of Understanding IP Strategies

N.S. Rathore, S.M. Mathur and Anshul Rathi

Abstract

The main aim of the article is to identify the strengths, weaknesses, opportunities and threats of current IPR system in context to Indian regime and also to understand overall planning as well as important tactics and means to use IP legal protection system to fully safeguard one's legitimate rights and interests, obtain and maintain competitive edges, restrain competitors and seek optimal economic performance by selection of appropriate IP strategies. This article also proposes ways to select IP strategy based on BCG matrix and product mix.

Keywords: Intellectual property, IP strategies, SWOT, Product mix

Introduction

The term intellectual property describes the set of different regulatory concepts that control the production and usage of intellectual objects. The three main concepts are patents, copyright and trademarks, but other special regimes for specific types of objects – for example, geographical identifiers, or industrial designs – exist.

Often a distinction is made between copyright, which starts automatically at the creation of the object and does not require any special registration or check, and the other concepts, that are aimed at protecting the commercial exploitation of ideas, and are subject to application for registration and to the verification of some requirements. In all cases, these instruments grant exclusive monopoly for a limited time on some rights over the intellectual object.

Patent is a highly technical type of intellectual property. Creation, use and maintenance of this type of asset requires skilled personnel with three different backgrounds: technology, business and legal. In this short article, some light will be shed on how a company's management should take advantage of this legal right to safely expand their market reach, protect their market and use defensive or offensive strategies against competitors when needed.

Indian IP: A SWOT Analysis

Strength	**Weakness**
• The existence of IP network • Forward looking for collaboration • Potential to tap scientific & technology professionals • Creating wealth and job places. Thus representing a significant part of the GDP	• Transparency in patent prosecution • Indian corporation <10% IP filings • Limited IP awareness/knowledge • Inactivity of SMEs • Lack of available expertise • An overly high complexity of system
Opportunity	**Threat**
• Improvement of co-operation and co-ordination • Outsourcing hub : R&D/design/knowledge industry • Potential for Cross Over: Emerging breed of scientific & legal professionals • The improvement of education and information • The enforcement of the legal framework of IP protection	• Counterfeiting & Piracy • Absence of institutional reputation

Classification of IP Strategies

A. On the basis of scope of IP protection

1. Patent Strategy:
    i. Patent application strategy
    ii. Patent protection strategy
    iii. Patent licensing strategy
    iv. Patent transfer strategy

2. Trademark Strategy:
   - i. Trademark use strategy
   - ii. Trademark design and selection strategy
   - iii. Associated trademark strategy
   - iv. Defensive trademark strategy
3. Trade Secret Protection Strategy and Non Competition

B. On the basis of strategy implementation responding to market competition

1. Offensive IP strategy
2. Defensive IP strategy
3. Offensive-Defensive IP strategy

C. On the basis of stages of technological development of entreprises

1. Initial stage
2. Stalemate stage
3. Attacking stage

These strategies can be summarized in a table format as shown in Table 1.

Selection of IP strategies integrating BCG Matrix strategic orientation chart

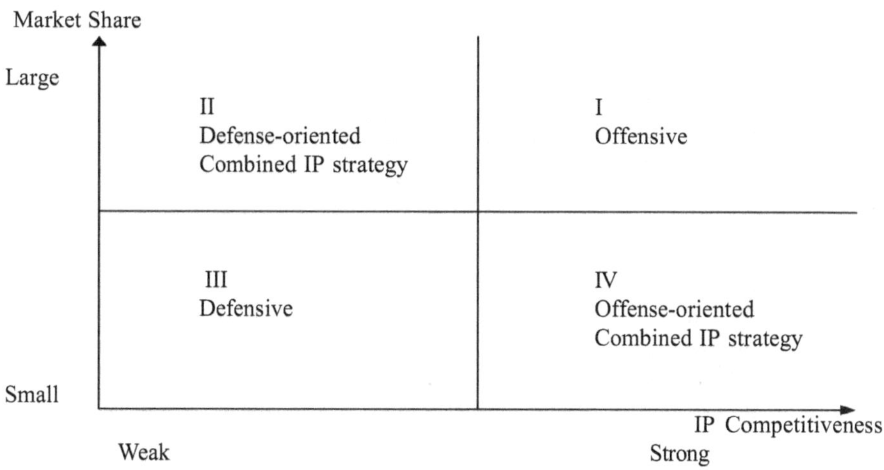

Fig.1: IP Strategic Orientation Chart

Table 1: Classification of Corporate IP Strategies

Types of Strategy		Implementation
Corporate patent strategies	Offensive patent strategies	Basic patent strategy, patent network strategy, patent salestrategy, patent buying strategy, patent feedback strategy,patent-product strategy, patent-trademark strategy, patentinvestment and acquisition strategy, patent litigation strategy, patent-standard strategy
	Defensive patent strategies	Strategy for cancelling the rival's patent, publicationstrategy, cross-licensing strategy, strategy to use invalidpatents, round-the-barrier patent strategy and basic patentexpiry strategy
	Offensive-Defensive patent strategies	Combinations of the above strategies according to actualconditions
	Technology import and export patent strategy	Patent buying strategy, cross-licensing strategy, directintroduction strategy and innovative introduction patentstrategy, patent cooperation strategy, patent franchisestrategy, compensatory trade strategy with patent andtechnology transfer
Corporate trademark strategies		Trademark use strategy, trademark design and selectionstrategy, trademark prompt registration strategy, associated trademark strategy, defensive trademark strategy, trademark trade name integration strategy, trademark image strategy, trademark competition strategy, trademark advertising strategy, trademark licensing strategy, renowned trademark strategy
Corporate trade secret strategies		Trade secret protection strategy, non-competition
Corporate IP management strategies		Setting up a corporate IP management agency

I quadrant

These types of enterprises are star enterprises with high technology capacities, strong IP competitiveness, high market share and strong marketing ability. Enterprise with strong technology development capability and financial strength may establish their own research institute and focus on independent innovation. On the one hand, they should patent their technology, obtain independent IP rights and continuously develop new technology; on the other hand, they should industrialize the technology and explore the market

II quadrant

These enterprises have moderate scales, average IP competitiveness as well as weak technological innovation capacity and competitiveness yet flexible mechanism, strong resilience and marketing ability as well as high market share. They are cash cows, and can adopt defense-oriented combined IP strategy supplemented by trademark and brand strategies to gain IP competitiveness.

III quadrant

These enterprises have small scales, limited funds, low IP competitiveness and relatively small market share. It is difficult to turn their technology into IP. They may adopt defensive patent strategies, positively introduce technology from other enterprises or use invalid patents. They can also research and develop IP jointly with other enterprises or research institutes, so as to improve their technology capacity.

IV quadrant

These enterprises feature strong IP competitiveness, relatively strong technological innovation capacity yet inadequate marketing ability and low market share. They are enterprises with unbalanced strength. Therefore, it is critical to enhance their market share by mainly implementing trademark and brand strategy while adopting offense-oriented combined IP strategy.

IP strategies based on Product Mix

Start-ups and small companies typically have a single product. They usually cannot afford working on several products concurrently. They will eventually hit and win, or miss and demise. However, the IP strategy is different for medium and large companies as they need and can afford to work on several products in order to insure their future success. As the Boston Consulting Group (BCG) Matrix illustrates, the best product mix for these companies is comprised of three groups of products: question marks (still in R&D); stars (fastest growing products); and cash cows (low margin, big market and steady). Each of these products must be successful in their own business life cycle in order for the company to remain successful in the long term. Products will have a different profit margin and market share in each quadrant of the BCG matrix. The IP strategy, new filing, and patent acquisition pace must also align with the product cycle to further enable the company's success in the future.

Each type of product moves along the traditional S-curve product cycle until it phases out. Depending on the spot on the S curve, there will be a different IP strategy that companies need to pursue. Deviation from the right strategy may endanger both future growth and market share for that product.

Question mark products are the ones that are still in the R&D phase. The future market, growth and all business factors are more speculation than facts. However, to guarantee future success, IP strategy and filing has to start here. In this phase, the company is either the pioneer or is trying to catch up with competition by researching and developing the same product. Patents can be obtained organically through in-house innovation, or non-organically by acquisition from others, or a combination of both. The filing pace is high, since the new product's patents will likely have broad claims with good coverage of the product. It is important to keep a fast and steady filing pace at this stage.

If the question mark products succeed in the market, at some point they will climb up the S-curve and enjoy a fast adoption by market. Products will become the "star" products of the company with high growth and high margin. At this time, competition has noticed the importance of this emerging product so they will use all forces to catch up and compete. The right IP strategy is to continue

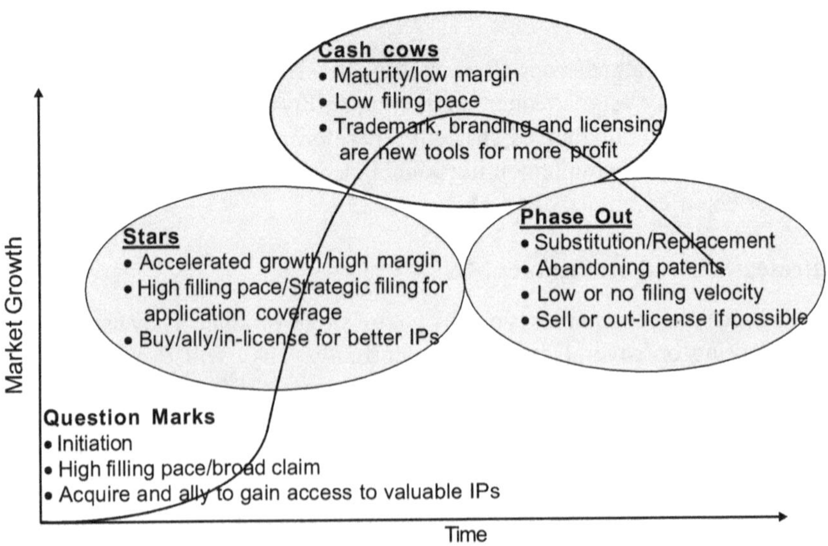

Fig.2: IP strategy: Product life cycle

filing at a high pace. At this point, patents will most likely have narrower claims (as long as the initial patent work has covered the most important aspects of the product) and mostly targeted towards specific applications. An IP portfolio has to be enforced in all possible ways which means in-house innovation as well as acquisition and in-licensing.

At the top of the S-curve, the product reaches maturity where it enjoys a big market while profit margins gradually decline and the product becomes a commodity. At this point, resources must be used and focused towards the next generation of the product rather than keeping the fast filing pace. Issued patents and existing applications most likely cover all important features of the product. Filing a new application is like stepping on a land mine as most likely the claims will get rejected or narrowed to a point that does not add any value. Although we still need to keep an eye on filing by selectively filing new applications where we see a weakness or gap in our portfolio, we should focus most of our resources towards other methods of marketing such as branding. Trademarks may bring more value in this phase. As profit margins are gradually declining, it may make more sense to out-license the technology which will result in relinquishing part of the market share to competitors in exchange for royalty income. This strategy will open up room in the company's manufacturing capacity for higher margin products.

Usually, at the end of the maturity phase, a product may be phased out because newer or better replacement products have emerged, or because of a shift in consumer desires. At this stage, IP managers need to continuously review the portfolio and abandon patents that do not cover any existing or future products. New filing almost does not make any sense. However, smart licensing may still be valid if patents are broad enough to cover applications in other industries or segments.

Conclusion

For an enterprise, the core of formulating and implementing IP strategy is to analyze the enterprise' IP competitiveness according to its internal and external environments, and then to select a suitable strategy model. Guided by its overall strategic objective, it should determine its IP strategic objective based on analysis of internal and external environments of its IP, select a suitable IP strategy and strategy combination, and strengthen the implementation, management and monitoring of its IP strategy.

4

Patent and the Issues on Technology Transfer

D.R. Agarwal

Technology transfer is an important commercial tool for leveraging and optimizing the value of intangible assets in the present era of globalization which has deepen the process of integration of the economic resources including the free movement of goods, merchandise, services, capital and intellectual property rights. This economic integration is facilitated by a legal framework of World Trade Organization (WTO) under various agreements including the Trade Related Aspects of Intellectual Property Rights (TRIPS). There are other International Institutions i.e., World Intellectual Property Organization (WIPO), World Customs Organizations (WCO) and United Nations Conference on Trade and Development (UNCTAD) to regulate and provide guidance for the protection and enforcement of IPRs. The present global economy is geared and triggered by knowledge and almost 80 % of the global wealth comes from knowledge based intangible assets and helps optimization of the limited global resources. Technology transfer is a tool for leveraging the value of IPRs and also for sharing knowledge around the world. Knowledge is weightless and in today's era, knowledge is driven by Information and Communication Technology (ICT) which adds to productivity in all aspects of economic life.

The term "Technology transfer" broadly connotes transfer of knowledge from one legal entity to another legal entity within and outside the national territories of the legal owner of the Patent holder at a consideration, known as license fees or technical fees or royalty. This may happen as a part of Foreign Direct Investment (FDI) or as a part of pure technological collaboration. In other words, Transfer of Technology (TOT) and Technology Commercialization allows the transfer of the technology by a patent holder to a user for further development and exploitation of the technology into new products, processes, applications, material or services. Patent provides an exclusive right to the patentee to exclude others from using an invention without his consent and the technology transfer is the process to include the licensee as the legal user without infringing the rights of the patentee. The exclusive right granted to a patentee is the right to prevent others from making, using, selling, or distributing the patented invention without his permission. The technology transfer allows the user to use the patented technology with the consent of the patent holder.

Lab to land is the ultimate goal of any invention. Technology transfer is the tool to reach to this goal by filling the invention-investment gap. In simple words, it can be understood as converting an idea into an asset. Thus an idea conceived and formulated at the laboratory stage is to ultimately meet the test of techno-commercial viability. Whereas the invention of an idea is the job of a scientist to convert it into a commercial asset useful for the consumer and here the society plays the job of an entrepreneur. The term creative destruction sometimes known as "Schumpeter's gale" gets fully reflected when a new technology is invented and transferred for wealth creation through technology transfer. Solow (1957), was able to demonstrate this effect based on data of United States economy from 1909-49, where only 12.5 percent of the increase of per capita output could be traced to increased use of capital and remaining 87.5 percent residual was attributed to technical change [1]. Technology Transfer is an important issue in the field of Intellectual Property Rights. There is often a Technology Transfer Office (TTO) attached to the research institutions or the Universities which deal with the Technology Transfer and act as a bridge between the research Institutions which are engaged in the inventions and the industries which are ready for making investments in such inventions and technologies. Technology Transfer thus facilitates purchase of technology either from the foreign market or from the domestic market in exchange of payment in the form of royalty or one-time upfront payment for the license to use such technology on exclusive or non-exclusive basis. It is therefore important to understand various issues which are relevant in the process of technology transfer as listed below:-

- Process of technology transfer
- Identification of potential licensees
- Buyer's perspective: Due diligence
- Seller's perspective: Licensing or outright sale- Different options, royalties, valuation etc.
- Legal issues

We will examine all the above issues briefly herein under

[1]. Source: "Technological innovation and theories of regional development" Matthew A. Zook

Technology transfer process

Technology transfer broadly takes place by the below mentioned stages:-

1. Research
2. Development of invention
3. Invention disclosure
4. Proof of concept
5. Determining the commercial viability
6. Patenting
7. Commercialization by means of technology transfer or of self use
8. Technology transfer by either lump sum sale or by licensing
9. Licensing may be exclusive or non exclusive

Different stages of technology transfer

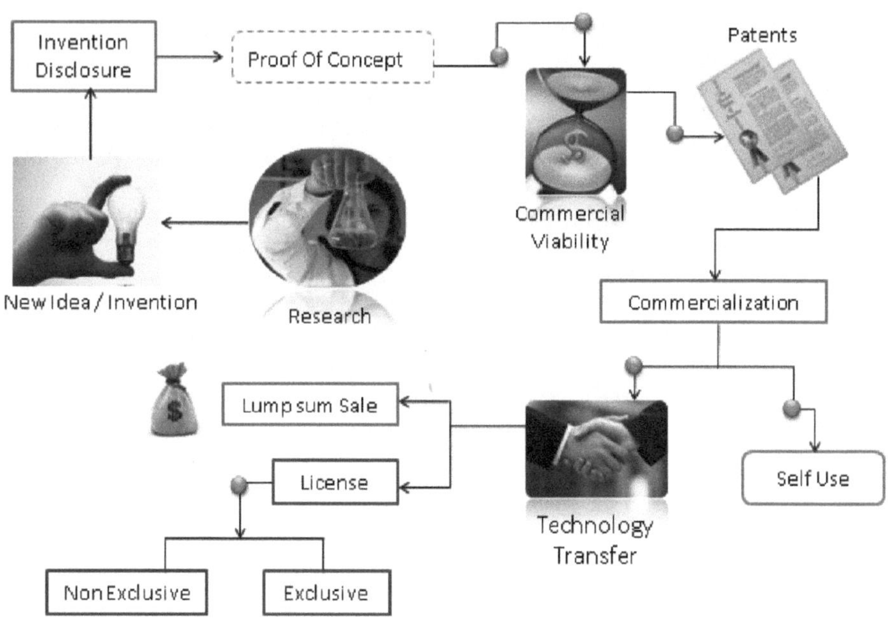

Technology Transfer – management process

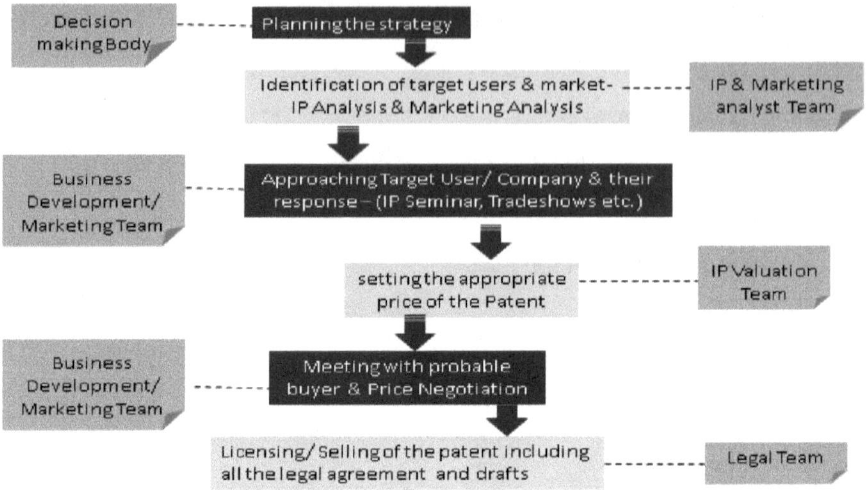

The technology transfer process - work flow

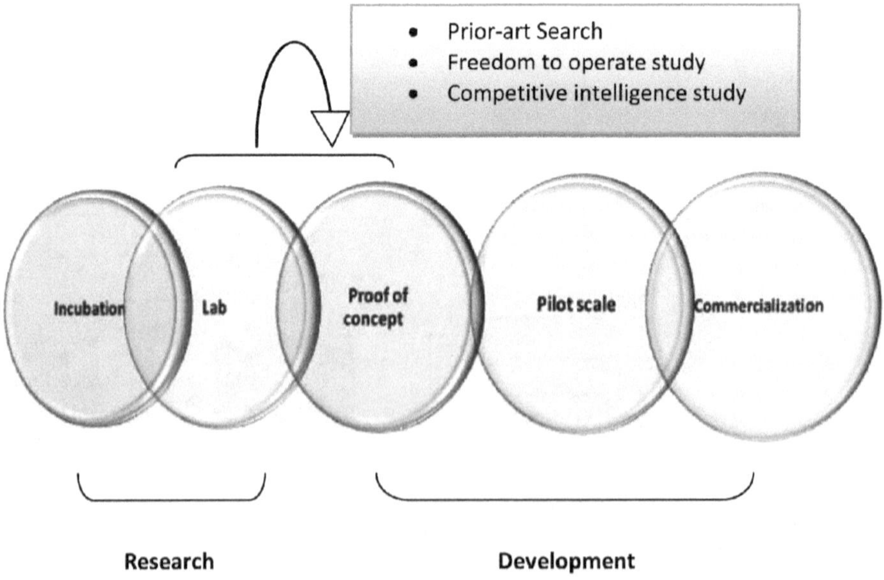

Research Development_Tasks involved in the Technology Transfer Process include

In Technology Transfer patentee retains patent rights to its technologies and licensee will be granted only a license to use the technology.

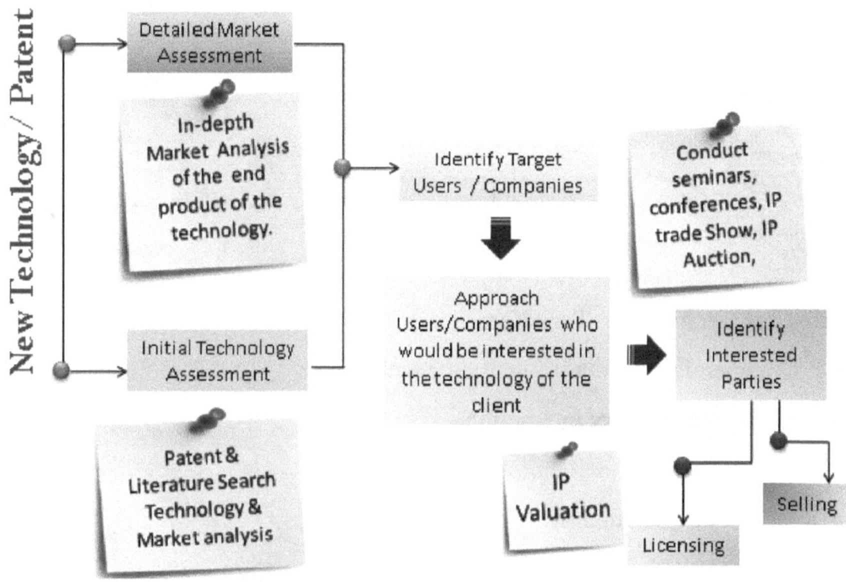

Initial Technology Assessment is done by means of patent and literature search and through market analysis which includes in-depth market analysis of the end product of the technology. Depending upon the nature and scope of technology, target users or companies are identified and approached. When a company has indicated interest for licensing the invention, call or meeting between both parties to discuss each others requirement, are arranged. Before disclosing the invention, Non Disclosure Agreement is signed. If the buyer company is convinced then second round of meeting is arranged between buyer and seller. Price negotiation begins and depending on the mode of technology transfer, price and term are fixed. Finally licensing or selling of technology takes place.

Identification of Potential Licensee

Licensing of patents involve a sequence of processes which includes identification of potential licensees, patent assertion, drafting of licensing agreement. In order to benefit the society, the lab inventions need to be successfully commercialized. Thus lab will get support from the licensing income generated for the future research only by identifying industry partners to sponsor Lab research.

The process involved

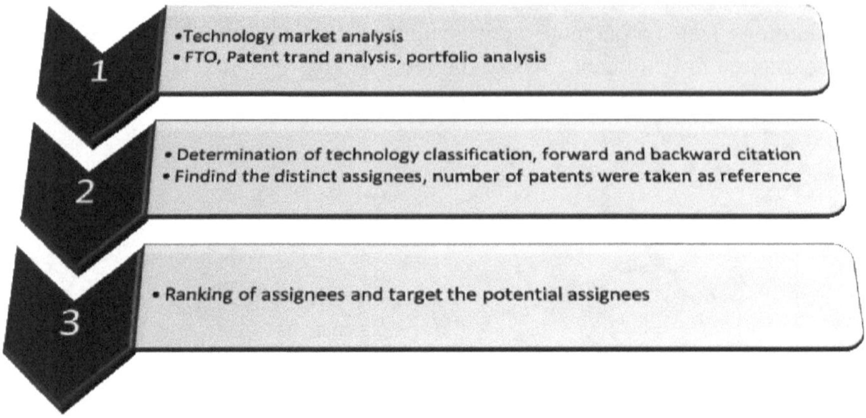

Routes for Technology Transfer

- Commercialization through new ventures
- Academia-industry interaction
- Pre-competitive, collaborative R&D
- Industrial Consultancy
- Sponsored Research

Pre-patent Licensing

Pre-patent licensing is an excellent option for the inventors which allow both licensor and licensee to avoid costly international filing of patents where there is uncertainty over the scope or likelihood of patent protection for those countries. An agreement in the pre-patent licensing, in its early stage much before the actual patent is being filed, ensures that costly duplication of R&D is avoided where there is already a technology existed with an earlier publication. The mode, form and nature of cooperation (e.g., exclusive versus non-exclusive licensing, royalty rates, the average number of patent citations for each patent's technological category, the number of citations received by the patent in question, the patents referred by a same assignee etc) are required parameters to be considered in this regard. This further prevents possible infringement, and finding out the possibility of 'inventing around' for the technology in question.

Licensing term and related transactions

Terms of each license depends upon:

1. Market value of the target technology in the relevant industrial sector

2. Products associated with the technology and competitiveness

Licenses broadly have at least following **three monetary** transactions:

- *License issue fee:* this is due upon execution of the agreement;
- *Running royalty:* depends upon the percentage of sales; and
- *Minimum annual royalties:* when a company is unable to meet minimum annual sales targets, the license term will be terminated, or will be converted to a non-exclusive license.

So this is very important to consider the Performance of the licensed technology by continuously marketing and selling of the product in order to keep the licensing status viable.

Buyer's Perspective

Due Diligence Issues related to Technology transfer

Patent due diligence involves analysis of the patents, the technology trend, the potential competitors, validation of entire business opportunity and detailed explanation of title to the assets to be transferred. A complete IP due diligence report envisages the followings (i) the nature of agreement fee and royalties to be paid are reasonable and worthwhile, and (ii) no potential risk of infringement involved. There is enough technology gap in between the existing competitors in this existing field of technology, helps to detect (i) ownership, (ii) validity, (iii) expiry date, (iv) disputes and other rights associated with the technology to be transferred. There are various kinds of prior art searches conducted during IP due diligence process. It identifies current level of technical development in a particular field, pre existing research on a field of technology, potential players and emerging players in the same technological field, white space between the related technologies and the legal statuses of equivalent patents with their relevant reference patents, to find out the technology trend in a more efficient way.

Different searches carried out are

- **Novelty/Patentability Search:** It is performed before preparing a patent application in order to determine whether or not the invention will be patentable based on the grounds of novelty, non-obviousness and utility which are interpreted differently in different legislatures and judiciary systems of different countries.
- **Patentability Search (excluding Novelty):** It provides information whether an invention is patentable or not by analyzing the claims of a patent application so that an applicant can suitably amend his application.
- **State-of The Art Search:** State of the art search results can provide a

basis for making critical market decisions. These results can also be used as a navigation framework for product and process design.

- **Validity/Invalidity Search:** The sole idea is to find prior art that is relevant in terms of the validity of the CLAIMS of the subject patent. Though the interest for validity search is for the issued patent, filing date (patent term) holds a very important aspect in the validity search process.
- **Freedom to Operate Search:** It identifies potential patent barriers in order to practice or use an invention or commercialize the products or technologies. The search involves finding and understanding the claims of third-party's in-force valid patents to determine whether the claims are infringing the claims of the patent of interest. The FTO analysis facilitates the launching of the product with the application of the new technology as a due diligence effort to avoid risk of infringement and also ensures the potential licensee about the novelty aspect of the technology.
- **Patent Competitive Intelligence:** It is about finding the existing competitors working in a technology. Technical know how disclosed in the various prior arts are the mile stones for the pipe line products coming in this field. The key players, their products, competitors and the scope of future development are highlighted to guide the researchers. This exercise also ensures the potential licensee about the competitiveness of the technology.

Seller's perspective

Royalty issues in technology transfer

Royalties received by the patentee for the licensing of the patent in a patent infringement lawsuits where courts need to decide the followings: nature and scope of the license as exclusive or nonexclusive, commercial relationship between the licensor and licensee, territory of business, competitors in the same territory in the same field of technology, duration of the patent and the term of the license, potential benefit to those for whom it is intended to be used and so on.

The utility and advantages of the patent property over the technologies already disclosed in the prior art, is required to be determined to make a reasonable profit and acceptable by the patentee who is willing to grant a license.

License fee, Equity (especially if licensee is a start-up company), Royalty on net sales by licensee and its sub-licensee (sometimes royalty per product sold), Percentage of non-royalty sublicense income (e.g. sublicense fees), Minimum annual royalties or maintenance fees are of concerned in order to determine the royalty.

Economic life and legal life of technology

Sometimes the economic life of a technology may be smaller or larger than the patented legal life of technology, depending on the life cycle or the obsolescence factors of the respective area in technology.

In case of Information Technology, where the changes are taking place very fast, the economic life of the technology may be of 5 or 6 years whereas the patent life will be of 20 years and therefore the valuation of the technology for determining royalty will be guided by the economic life and not by the legal life.

No government approval and payments for technology transfer under the automatic route

_Indian companies who are engaged in technology transfer with foreign firms, who are paying royalty to those foreign firms for technology transfer, will no longer be required to take government approval. This facilitates more investment and transfer of technologies to India. The department of Industrial Policy and promotion (DIPP) in 2009, made all the payments for technology transfer under the automatic route without any ceiling limit. It is important to mention that, all such payments will be subjected to Foreign Exchange Management (Current Account Transactions) Rule 2000.

Technology transfer and working of patents

In India, section 146 of the Patent Act, 1970, empowers the controller to obtain the details of actual working of the patents from the Patentee or Licensee at periodic intervals in form 27. The aforesaid objectives are also stated in section 83 of the Patent Act which inter-alia includes the followings:

a. that patents are granted to encourage inventions and to secure that the inventions are worked in India on a commercial scale and to the fullest extent that is reasonably practicable without undue delay;

b. that they are not granted merely to enable patentees to enjoy a monopoly for the importation of the patented article;

c. that the protection and enforcement of patent rights contribute to the promotion of technological innovation and to the transfer and dissemination of technology, to the mutual advantage of producers and users of technological knowledge and in a manner conducive to social and economic welfare, and to a balance of rights and obligations.

Modes of Technology transfer

There are different modes of technology transfer existing in the current international system includes Licensing, Foreign direct investment, Sale, Turnkey contracts, Acquisition of equipment etc.

Licensing

Licensing may be defined as the process in which an owner of an intangible asset, transfers the right to use that asset to another, for a price, while retaining ownership of that asset. Generally the owner of a technology protected by patents or trade secrets or both gives another the right to use that technology to manufacture given product(s).

Assignment of IP Rights

When the owner of an IP, transfers all the exclusive rights to a patented invention or any other protected IP, without any restriction in time or any other condition to another person for a particular price, it is said that an "assignment" of such rights has taken place.

The Turn-Key Project

The word "Turn-key" means ready for immediate use. In this mode of technology transfer, different entities are responsible for setting up a plant or equipment and for putting it into operation. It's a project which is constructed by a developer and sold or turned over to a buyer in a ready-to-use condition.

Foreign direct investment (FDI)

FDI may be defined as a long term involvement of a country A with another country B which usually involves participation in management, joint-venture, transfer of technology and "know-how".

Acquisition of Equipment

The commercial transfer and acquisition of technology can take place with the sale purchase of equipment and other capital goods. Sales and purchases of capital goods and their import into the country can be considered, in a sense, technology transfers transactions.

Licensing

IP licensing can be either exclusive or non-exclusive. The exclusivity may be for the product, field or territory or the combination of any of these. The owner of IP may also look for other mode of optimizing the revenue by retaining the right to manufacture and to grant exclusive right of marketing or by licensing manufacturing right to one party and marketing right to another and for selling right to yet another party. There can be other mode of commercialisation through venture capitalists or through a joint venture. Franchising is another mode of licensing where each licence is a part of a larger network with uniformity in application of technology or the brand. The types of licenses followed or recognized in India are:

a. Express License
b. Statutory License
c. Implied License
d. Exclusive License
e. Non- Exclusive License

Concept of licensing in the patent technology transfer

Licensing of technology is a multifaceted and serious process involving legal, technical, financial, and other policy related matters. Licensing negotiation is a key regulating factor determining the business expectations of both parties. Expressions, ideas, innovations and creation of human mind are intangible properties which are protected by law through the intellectual property system. The National Innovation Initiative (NII) defines innovation as, "the intersection of invention and insight, leading to the creation of social and economic value" (Council on Competitiveness, 2004). Innovation is being further defined as, "the use of new technological knowledge, and/or new market knowledge, employed within a business model that can deliver a new product or service to customers who will purchase at a price that will provide profits" (Warren & Susman, 2004).

As an immovable property, they are tradable assets. Licensing, grants the right of the owner to another person who will use this asset while continuing to retain ownership of that asset to the owner. In return the person using this asset will have to pay the royalty to the actual owner. Licensing creates a source of income, publicizes the technology to its best possible usage and acts as a potential catalyst for further business development and commercialization of the target technology. University decisions on licensing a patented technology only to one company or to a group of companies are based on **two major factors**: (1) to choose what kind of licensing causing rapid commercialization; and (2) what kind of licensing supports the public interest. Other factors guiding the transfer of technology in universities, as per the survey of 75 different Technology Transfer Offices (TTOs) in U.S are illustrated in the table [1] below:

Center Priority	% of Centers
Releasing Technology for the Public Good	40%
Keeping Faculty Happy	24%
Maintaining Corporate Relationships	17%
Generation of Short-term Revenue	6%
Generation of Long-term Capital Gains	5%
Attracting Research Funding	4%
Protecting Intellectual Property	2%

[1]*Source*: "Models for university technology transfer: resolving conflicts between mission and methods and the dependency on geographic location"

Some key negotiation points in Technology Transfer deals

1. Determining of scope of the license - Exclusivity, duration, enforcement rights are the key issues to be considered
2. Determining of the initial license fee - The amount of fee payable up-front.
3. Royalty payments to be fixed - The royalty calculation can be based on sales revenues, units, profits.
4. Due diligence report, audit rights - Licensor must have an access to measure the sales or other figures in order to assess royalties from the licensee and to verify the accuracy of the report generated.

Technology transfer and commercialization

Commercialization is the key tool for transferring technologies. An effective commercialization and commercial success depends mainly on few factors viz.

1. Technical Development

The technical knowhow, time, raw materials, and personnel required to reduce the technology to practice to the persons ordinarily skilled in the art and protect their rights to the resulting product.

2. Regulatory Compliance

The safety and regulatory authorities needed to examine and quality check the final product's utility and safety, to satisfy the federal regulatory requirements and to minimize or manage risks associated with the products.

3. Manufacturing Requirements

The optimum manufacturing conditions, trained man power and equipment needed to make the product.

4. Market Development

Before the commercialization of the products potential users of the target technology should be found out to for successful marketing of the product, considering the nature of the product, size of potential market, means for successful penetration into the market, expected sales, advantages over existing competing products and the cost and time of promoting the product.

5. Financial Feasibility

The production cost, development costs, operating expenses in relation to sales potential, net profits, potential liabilities, and associated risk, avoidance of infringement and costly litigation and return on investment.

There are **various means** by which knowledge gets transferred from the public research system to the private sectors:

1. **Public-private partnerships (PPPs):** This initiative during post-2005 has been taken up by many new consortium-based approaches. In the ICAR system, the National Agricultural Innovation Project (NAIP) actively involved with the private sector, bringing innovations from innovators thought to the practical platform, with each consortium addressing specific technology gaps in the entire value chain.
2. **Scientific papers, publications and other literatures** by the academic scientists are the means of knowledge transfer in the public sector where scientific research is communicated through informal discussions, interviews, conference, tradeshows and presentations.
3. **Technology commercialization** in the public research system includes creation of IP cells, appointment of IP personnel, and through intensive IP awareness programmes.

CSIR, ICMR, ICAR, Indian Institutes of Technology (IITs) in Bombay and Delhi and the Indian Institute of Science (IISc) Bengaluru are few of the eminent public research systems in India.

New Millennium India Technology Leadership Initiative (NMITLI) is one of the largest public-private partnerships in R&D in India, started by the Government of India, and monitored through the CSIR. NMITLI catalyzes innovation centered scientific and technological developments as a vehicle to attain for Indian industry a global leadership position. NMILTI is interested to discover and harmonize the strengths of publicly funded R&D institutions, academia and industry, and through this process, catalyze scientific and technological innovation in some selected niche theme areas. In NMITLI almost all projects are built in a public-private partnership mode. (*Source*: NMITLY, CSIR)

The purpose and benefits of technology transfer includes the following

- It promotes the use of technology developed by effective commercialization to benefit society.
- It increases the value of research program relevancy and value.
- It generates an opportunity for the federal researchers to partner with the private sector, leverage resources, and share ideas in a defined environment.
- It helps the researchers to generate and earn royalty income from their creation.

Technology transfer and technical knowhow

It is very important to understand the distinction between the term "technology" which is embedded in a patent or in an IPR, which is transferred and the term "technical know how" which is necessary to implement the technology or to put it to use. Know-how means technical data, formulae, standards, technical information, specifications, processes, methods, code books, raw materials, as well as all information, knowledge, assistance, trade practices and secrets, and improvements thereto, divulged, disclosed, or in any way communicated to the Licensee under this agreement, unless such information was, at the time of disclosure, or thereafter becomes part of the general knowledge or literature which is generally available for public use from other lawful sources. The burden of proving any information disclosed hereunder is not confidential information shall rest on the licensee. A contract for technology transfer can either be a licence agreement or a know-how agreement. The licence agreement normally refers to the licensing of intellectual property rights such as patents, trade marks, copyrights, etc. whereas a know-how agreement involves the transfer of information or skills which have not received statutory recognition. [1]

P atent Valuation and technology transfer issues

Valuation plays an important role is the process of technology transfer. The method to be chosen for technology transfer depends on the kind of technology and the party in question (technology buyer or a technology seller). In this regard, the potential market size, territory of product launch, potential competitors and the adoption rate for the product are important issues to be considered.

Most commonly the discounted cash flow method is followed, which calculates the present value of future revenues. In general there are three traditional models for valuation i.e. the cost method, the market value method, and the income method. However keeping in mind the complexities associated with valuation there are certain modern application methods like the real option.

[1]. Source: Wikipedia valuation model and the simulation model which is used for the purpose of valuation of patents. There are other methods which are followed viz. hybrid approaches, royalty rate method.

Patent Troll' and 'Patent Sharks'

One of the recent malpractice of the patent right is by virtue of purchasing the patents from the patentees in financial distress and enforcing the same against purported infringers. This device is popularly known as "Patent Troll" and is used by Non Practicing Entity (NPE) or Non Manufacturing Patentee (NMP). However, the restriction for grant of a patent for software, as per the provision of section 3(k) of Indian Patent Act, 1970 provide relief from the attack of Patent Trolling to some extent.

A similar version of the above kind of malpractice is also adapted by 'Patent Sharks'. The firms in technology sector face great difficulties from the Patent sharks. These are the firms, who acquire various patents by means of acquisitions, licensing agreements or through R&D and these acquired patents are kept on hold and hidden from the public domain. In order to escape from these patent sharks, tech firms should maintain standardized technologies so that they can add or remove technological features in order to make them patentable and reform their R&D processes instead of relying on legal remedies, through Freedom to Operate (FTO) Analysis.

Legal Issues

In India the agreement for transfer of technology either by way of licensing or by way of one time sale is guided by the provisions of Section 2(h) of the Indian Contract Act, 1872. The Indian Contract Act provides that any legally enforceable agreement is a contract and therefore an agreement for licensing or assignment of technology has to satisfy the requirements of the Indian Contract Act, 1872. In other words, any agreement for transfer of technology has to be made by the free consent of parties competent to contract, for a lawful consideration and with a lawful object and also has to be made in such a manner that it is not declared void under Section 10 of the Indian Contract Act, 1872. Broadly these conditions for a legal agreement are common in all the countries.

Meaning of Legal Assignments

Legal Assignments provides the assignee all the rights of the patent for which he is entitled to be registered as the proprietor of the patent. The deed of assignment of the patent needs to be filed at the patent office at the time of filing or within six months of filing of the patent application. Generally if the inventor is working in an organization, he is paid for his work and there is an inbuilt clause in the letter of appointment that all kinds of Intellectual property developed by him during the course of employment will be the property of the employer and thus the consideration value shown in the deed of assignment is very nominal. However in other commercial transactions of technology transfer by way of assignment is through a registered deed of assignment which is executed on a stamp paper by paying requisite stamp fees and registration fees. Generally a non-disclosure and Confidential Agreement is signed before execution of the deed of assignment. In contrast, Joint Venture Agreements is a legal contract between two or more companies assuring to co-operate and combine their resources for a project or series of projects, but do not wish to create a single business entity. There are various other modes of technology commercialization including merger and acquisition, existing technology of one enterprise gets transferred to the other enterprise through an order of the court.

Technology transfer and Indian Patents Act

In India, section 140 of the Indian Patents Act, 1970 provides for avoidance of certain restrictive conditions in the technology transfer licensing agreements and if an agreement contains such restrictions, they are considered unlawful and void. However, section 3(5) of the Indian competition Act 2002 provides for certain exemptions to restrictions on transfer of patented technology if imposition of such conditions are reasonable for protection of any rights which have been conferred or may be conferred to the licensor under various provisions of IPR laws in India including the copyright Act, 1957 and the patent Act 1970. Section 83(c) and Section 83(f) of Indian Patents Act, 1970, speaks about endorsement of technology innovation, technology transfer and prevention of exploitation of patent rights to unreasonably restrain international transfer of technology. This is in compliance with Article 7 of TRIPS.

Section 70 of the Indian Patents Act, 1970, allows the patentee to assign, grant licenses under, or otherwise deal with the patent and to give effectual receipts for consideration for any such assignment, license or dealing. Thus, it may be said that all technology transfer agreements either through assignments or through licensing have to comply with the various laws of the host country and the home country.

Grant of Compulsory License under Section 84 of Indian Patents Act, 1970

Section 84 states that at any time after the expiration of three years from the date of the grant of a patent, any person interested may make an application to the controller for grant of compulsory license on patent on any of the following grounds namely

a. that the reasonable requirements of the public with respect to the patented invention have not been satisfied

b. that the patented invention is not available to the public at a reasonably affordable price or

c. that the patented invention is not worked in the territory of India.

In March, the government had allowed Hyderabad-based Natco Pharma to manufacture and sell a generic version of cancer-treatment drug Nexavar at a price, over 30 times lower than charged by its patent-holder Bayer Corporation. The compulsory licence was granted to Natco by India Patents Office under Section 84 of the Indian Patent Act, which is in compliance with the TRIPS agreement of the World Trade Organisation.

Natco was allowed to sell the drug at a price not exceeding Rs 8,880 for a pack of 120 tablets required for a month's treatment as compared to a staggering Rs 2.80 lakh per month charged by Bayer for its patented Nexavar drug. (Source: Business standard)

Technology Transfer and Taxation issues

Transfer of technology involving cross-border transactions also involves application of transfer pricing regulations under the taxation laws of various countries. Provisions for taxation of IP in India include:

- Income Tax Act, 1961
- Sales of Goods Act, 1930
- Value Added Tax (VAT)
- Customs Tariff Act, 1975 (CT Act)
- Central Excise Act, 1944
- Service Tax (ST)

Indian Income Tax Act 1961 has embodied Special Provisions relating to avoidance of tax with relation to international transactions having regard to the arm's length price. The term "arm's length price" and the term "international transaction" have a separate meaning under chapter X of the Indian Income Tax Act 1961. An arm's length price means a price which is applied or proposed to be applied in a transaction between persons other than associated enterprises, in uncontrolled conditions. According to the provisions of Section-9(1)(vi) of Indian Income Tax Act, 1961 any income by the way of royalty is taxable in India as the same is treated as income deemed to accrue or arise in India. The term royalty has been defined under Explanation-2 of the aforesaid section and include the value of consideration for or in exchange of mainly of the followings:

1. The transfer of all or any rights (including the granting of a license) in respect of a patent, invention, model, design, secret formula or process or trade mark or similar property.
2. The transfer of all or any rights (including the granting of a license) in respect of any copyright, literary, artistic or scientific work including films or video tapes for use in connection with radio broadcasting, but not including consideration for the sale, distribution or exhibition of cinematographic films. However, one must remember to make the distinction between the income by way of royalty and income by way of fees for deemed income under the provisions of section 9(1)(vii) and has been mainly defined in Explanation 2 to the said section as below:

Explanation 2: "fees for technical services" means any consideration (including any lump sum consideration) for the rendering of any managerial, technical or consultancy services (including the provision of services of technical or other personnel) but does not include consideration for any construction, assembly, mining or like project undertaken by the recipient or consideration which would be income of the recipient chargeable under the head "Salaries".

The provisions of withholding tax on payment of royalty and fees for technical services to a non resident are applicable as per the provisions of section 195 and the Income Tax Act 1961 as per the rates prescribed either under the Income Tax Rules 1962 or the applicable rates as per the Double Taxation Treaties between Government of India and the other countries.

The above position of law as applicable for technology transfer as prescribed under Foreign Exchange Management Act, 2000 and under the Income Tax Act, 1961 must be borne in mind while advising any overseas clients for joint ventures or for foreign collaboration.

Foreign Technology Collaboration as per FDI Policies and Foreign Exchange Regulations of Government of India

A foreign company planning to set up business operations in India may:

- Incorporate a company under the Companies Act, 1956, as a Joint Venture or a Wholly Owned Subsidiary.
- Set up a Liaison Office / Representative Office or a Project Office or a Branch Office of the foreign company which can undertake activities permitted under the Foreign Exchange Management (Establishment in India of Branch Office or Other Place of Business) Regulations, 2000. [1]

Scope of Technology Collaboration

Automatic route under foreign technology collaboration specifies the disbursement terms for technical know how fees, for engineering service, royalty and payment for design and drawing.

RBI by means of distinct procedures and rules governs the procedures of payments for hiring of foreign technicians, deputation of Indian technicians abroad, testing of indigenous raw material and products in foreign countries.

[1] *Source*: RBI

Automatic Route

"FDI in sectors/activities to the extent permitted under automatic route does not require any prior approval either by the Government of India or RBI.

As per the latest Foreign Exchange Management (Current Account Transaction) (Amendment) Rules 2010, Notified dated 5th May 2010, G.S.R. 382(E) for FDI, no permission from Government of India or FIPB is required for technology collaboration for the formation of joint venture company in India, under Automatic Route.

Amendment Rules 2010 specifically says that "In the Foreign Exchange

Management (Current Account Transaction) (Amendment) Rules 2000, in Schedule-II, item number 8 and the entry relating thereto shall be omitted", which means that there remains no bar on payment of royalty in excess of 5% on local sales and 8% on exports and lump sum payment exceeding US$ 2 million. In the present case the parties do not require any permission or approval from Government of India or FIPB for investment in relation to the formation of joint venture for technological collaboration as set out in the share holding agreement.

Further, the requirement of registration of the agreement with the Regional Office of Reserve Bank of India has also been done away with. But the Authorized Dealer (AD) banks shall (subject to compliance with the provisions of Foreign Exchange Management (Current Account Transactions) Rules, 2000) exercise its delegated power (provided by RBI) to make payments for royalty, lump sum fee for transfer of technology and payment for use of trademark/brand name in terms of the foreign technology collaboration agreement entered by the Indian company with its foreign partners".

Technology Transfer and National Policy issues

India's recent development of technology transfer regulations aids foreign investors and their technology partners in India to promote more business. Technology Transfer across the borders involves lots of issues relating to the rules and guidelines on exchange controls, the anti-trust laws, the taxation laws and repatriation of royalties and license fees between the host country and the licensee countries. One has to also look into the existence of Tax Treaty and the bilateral investment treaty between the concerned two countries. The technology transfer may be either through a foreign technical collaboration or through a joint venture but under both the situation it is important to carefully examine the terms of the license agreement, especially the restrictions on improvements of the technology and the issues relating to joint ownership of the Intellectual Property along with the terms for payment or lump sum and the running royalty.

Each country has its own guideline for technology transfer. European Union regulates it by Article 81 of the EC Treaty to Technology Transfer agreements, whereby the licensor permits the licensee to exploit the licensed technology for the production of goods or services. The aim of Article 81 as a whole is to protect competition in the market and to avoid the abuses of monopolies. Technology is an input which is either a part of the product or a production process and therefore may affect competition in the existing market of the product or in an output market of a product where such technology is used to produce such goods or services. The European Union also provides for block exemption to certain categories of Technology transfer agreements which fulfills the conditions as set out in EC treaty to technology transfer agreements (TTBER).

Peoples Republic of China regulates Technology Transfers by Article 329 of the contract law which defines technology transfer in a broader concept, covering both assignments that involve the transfer of Intellectual Property and licensing that does not involve the transfer of Intellectual Property. It includes the assignments of Patent rights, patent licensing and transfer of knowhow or other Technology. Article 329 of the contract law states that any technology, which impedes technological progress or infringes upon the technological result of others, is null and void. There are additional rules regarding import and export of technologies and the following restrictions are banned in technology import contracts:

1. The condition to purchase unnecessary technology, raw materials, products, equipments or services;
2. Requiring transfer to pay royalties for technology for which relevant patent protection has expired;
3. Restricting the improvement or use of the subject technology by a transferee;
4. Restricting a transferee's right to obtain similar or competing technology from other sources.
5. Unreasonably restricting product output variety or sales price or export of goods.

"Licensing and Technology Transfer": Wipo

Role of patents for international IP-technology transfer for climate change mitigation in developing countries

The amount of greenhouse gas emissions resulting in climate changes depends substantially upon the wide variety of new mitigation and widespread dissemination of a large number of new technologies. Rapid economic growth in this knowledge based economical era has focused policy attention on the role of technology transfer and technology advancement in countries which are not in the leading role in facilitating the use of clean technologies. Energy and environment related innovation when protected under IP protection would cause detrimental consequences for global warming. Technologies developed related to climate change-related comprise a vast range of fundamentally. Patent protection offers only a restricted means for mitigating environmental externalities. The development and diffusion of technology regarding climate change creates an alarming challenge due to the presence of a "double externality". Technological know how addressed in the patents for the development of (green) technologies is characterized by non-excludability where the value of this technology will not be reduced by other actors. Recently the UN Framework Convention on Climate Change (UNFCCC) Ad-hoc Working Group on Long term Cooperative Action (AWG-LCA) has proposed specific IP-related regulations for the post-Kyoto framework on climate change. The regulations proposed by developing countries include patent pooling, royalty-free compulsory licensing of green technologies, excluding green technologies from patenting, and even revoking existing patent rights on green technologies (UNFCCC, 2010).

This regulation when implemented, it is noted that there are two groups of developing countries. In one hand, countries which are in the first group of emerging economies, such as Brazil, China, India, and Mexico and in the other hand in the second group there are a larger number of less developed countries. The issues related to the technology transfer and IPR protection of the green technologies for the group of emerging economies will be having a positive impact on the domestic development of technology and its transfer from developed economies which is not true in the case of less developed countries.

TRIPS and Technology transfer

Article 7 of the TRIPS sets out various objectives of the TRIPS agreement emphasizing the protection and enforcement of intellectual property rights in the promotion of technological innovation and technology transfer. More specifically it states that such technology transfer and dissemination should be for the joint benefit for innovators and users for social and economic welfare, and should create a balance of rights and obligations. It is clear that Article 7 recognizes creation of balance of rights and obligations. Both the private interest of the Patent holder and public interest in transfer or dissemination of technology should be given equal weightage. Further, Article 8(2) of the TRIPS provides member countries to adopt measures that prevent the misuse of intellectual property rights by right holders or the resort to practices which unfairly pin down trade or adversely affect the international transfer of technology. TRIPS also provides for exceptions to exclusive rights under Article 30 of the TRIPS Agreement allowing member states to provide limited exceptions to exclusive rights conferred by patents. "The obligation for developed countries to provide incentives for technology transfer is in Article 66.2. Least-developed countries want this requirement to be made more effective. In Doha, the member countries agreed that the TRIPS Council would "put in place a mechanism for ensuring the monitoring and full implementation of the obligations". The council adopted a decision setting up this mechanism in February 2003. It details the information developed countries are to supply by the end of the year, on how their incentives are functioning in practice". Articles 7, 8, 27.2, 31 TRIPS states that "despite the possibility of compulsory licensing, its benefits are limited inasmuch as the licensor cannot be obliged to transfer the corresponding know-how to the licensee" (Derclaye, 2008).

International patent exhaustion and bolar provision

Patent right is territorial in nature i.e. this right is conferred upon the country where it is granted. Article 6 of TRIPS agreement allows the countries to implement their own rules of exhaustion of patent rights. It determines the extent of the exhaustion of patent rights according to their national interests. In case of PCT application patent rights are exercised based on the countries where the PCT application is designated to. Under this provision patentee may file National phase applications in different designated countries within 30 to 31 months from the priority date or International Application date, whichever is earlier.

International patent exhaustion is based on the principle "First Sale Doctrine," Under this doctrine, patent holder's exclusive rights to control the use and sale of the patented article get exhausted, once an unrestricted, authorized sale of a patented article occurs in between the patent holder and the purchaser. The purchaser is then free to use or resell the patented article without any further control of the patentee.

In case of Bolar provision, a patented product can be used without the consent of the patent holder for procuring regulatory approval. Section 107A of the Indian Patents Act explains same kind of provision where certain acts will not be considered as infringing if the same are used for the development and submission of information required by the regulatory authorities for the approval of the patented product.

Effect of Bayh-Dole Act and the issues related to its compliance in India

The Bayh–Dole Act or Patent and Trademark Law Amendments Act is a 1980 US legislation, dealing with intellectual property to promote technology transfer by giving universities and research institutions ownership of patents resulting from federally funded research. In India, Protection and Utilization of Public Funded Intellectual Property Bill 2008 ("PUPFIP Bill") is an Indian version of 1980 US legislation. The idea behind the Bayh-Dole Act was that the research funded by the government and inventors to disclose their inventions rather than keep them as secrets. In 1980, over 28,000 unlicensed patents lay with the U.S. government.[1] Presently the Council of Scientific and Industrial Research (CSIR) has more than 5173 patents (counting both those in force and those under dispute), while only 222 patents are licensed (with 68 of them being under dispute). IIT-Kharagpur's TTO-equivalent (Sponsored Research & Industrial Consultancy division - SRIC) presently deals with Rs.300 crores through 850 projects of which nearly Rs. 5-15 crores are currently made through its patent portfolio.[2] Thus patents don't seem, on the face of things, to be the best way of ensuring technology transfer.

Inventor's share of royalties and income mentioned in Clause 8 of the PUPFIP Bill, is the most important clause of the proposed bill mentioned as follows: The royalties or income received by the Recipient(s) from the existing shall be shared with the inventor(s) in a proportion of 30%, net of expenses on IP protection and utilization, or where there is a written agreement between the Inventor and the Recipient(s), in the proportion prescribed in the written agreement, which shall not be less than 30% net of expenses on IP protection and utilization. Further,

Clause 14 of the proposed PUPFIP Bill gives preference to national industry which states that no Recipient(s) which receives title to any IP and no assignee of any such Recipient(s) shall grant to any person the exclusive right to use or sell any IP in India unless such person agrees that any products embodying the invention or produced through the use of the invention will be manufactured substantially in India.

[1] See So et al. and Thursby and Thursby, quoted in the National Knowledge Commission's letter to the Prime Minister.

[2] Prof. Vivekanandans' presentation "Patenting and Technology Transfer-the IIT Khargpur Experience"

Few Institutes facilitating the technology transfer process throughout the world:

- Science Forum for Intellectual and Industrial Property Services (SIPS) sipsmena.com/SIPS/Web/ContactUs.aspx
- The Center of Research and Technology at SABIC http://www.sabic.com/asia/en/ourcompany/contact/default.aspx
- Research and development centre – ARAMCO http://www. saudiaramco.com/en/home/innovation2/centers-of-research/research-and-development-center.html
- National Science Foundation (NSF) www.nsf.gov/
- Technology Information, Forecasting and Assessment Council (TIFAC) www.tifac.org.in/
- Ocean Tomo www.oceantomo.com/
- Organisation for Economic Co-operation and Development (OECD) www.oecd.org/

Conclusion

We have observed from the analysis as set out in the various paragraphs on the subject, that technology transfer is an essential part of the modern economy which is driven through knowledge. The basic tends to the economic globalism based upon the idea of sharing knowledge which helps in deriving values from innovation. Technology transfer helps in leveraging and optimizing the value of innovation through various modes of transfer of technology in the form of licensing and assignment. It is also being observed that technology involves a bundle of IP rights including Industrial design, Trademarks, technical know how and trade secrets and therefore it is very important to understand the implication while drafting the agreement for technology transfer.

The international legal frame work has created by various International organization have assured protection and enforcement of Intellectual Property but the degree of credibility for transfer of technology depends upon the level of risk of infringement and vis-a- vis the environment for protection and enforcement in the host country. The Foreign direct Investment (FDI) and increasing level of International trades in Goods and services has an inbuilt mechanism for technology transfer for improved efficiency of output and optimum allocation of the limited economic resources. Today the world is facing the problem of environment and energy security and therefore there is need for a cohesive dialogue amongst the countries through bilateral and multilateral negotiations for an uninterrupted flow of technology across the world.

References

Anthony Warren, Ralph Hanke, Daniel Trotzer, "Models for university technology transfer: resolving conflicts between mission and methods and the dependency on geographic location", Oxford Journals, Volume 1, Issue 2, Pp. 219-232.

Anthony D. So, Bhaven N. Sampat, Arti K. Rai, Robert Cook-Deegan, Jerome H. Reichman, Robert Weissman, Amy Kapczynski "Is Bayh-Dole Good for Developing Countries? Lessons from the US Experience" October 2008 Issue of PLoS Biology.

Jishnu L (2008) Does India need a Bayh-Dole Act? Patently absurd. Business Standard. Available: http://www.business-standard.com/india/s torypage.php?autono=328187. Accessed 16 September 2008.

Prof. Vivekanandan, presentation, Patenting and Technology Transfer-the IIT Khargpur Experience.

Book, Matthew A. Zook, Technological innovation and theories of regional development.

Michael Blakeney, Transfer of Technology and Devloping Nations, Volume 11, Issue 4, 1987

Bhaven N. Sampat, The Bayh-Dole Model in Developing Countries: Reflections on the Indian Bill on Publicly Funded Intellectual Property, policy brief Number 5, October 2009.

Policy on Inventions, Patents, and Technology Transfer, Faculty Handbook - Duke University, 2008.

Globalization Of R&D And Developing Countries, United Nations Conference On Trade And Development, Proceedings of the Expert Meeting Geneva, 24-26 January 2005.

5

Drafting of Complete Patent Specification with Case Study

Nidhi Bhatt and Anshul Rathi

The main purpose of this lecture note is to provide basic information on patent drafting skills and train applicants for drafting a patent in clear and concise manner.

We will see the components of Complete Specification through the following Case studey (1) of a solar water heater. The figures are provided below for reference and better understanding.

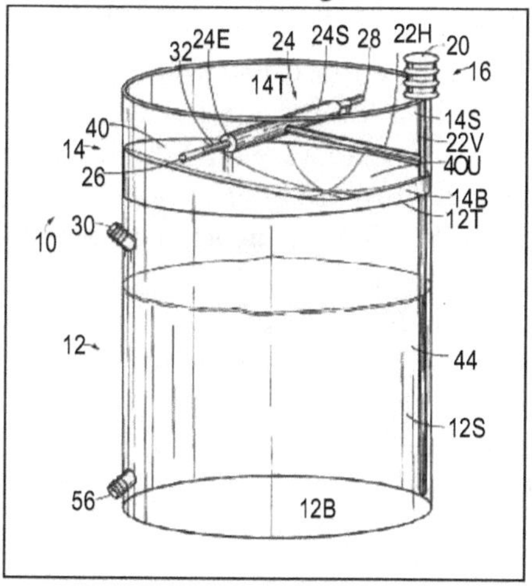

Fig. 1: Is perspective view of the solar water heater with a single parabolic reflector.

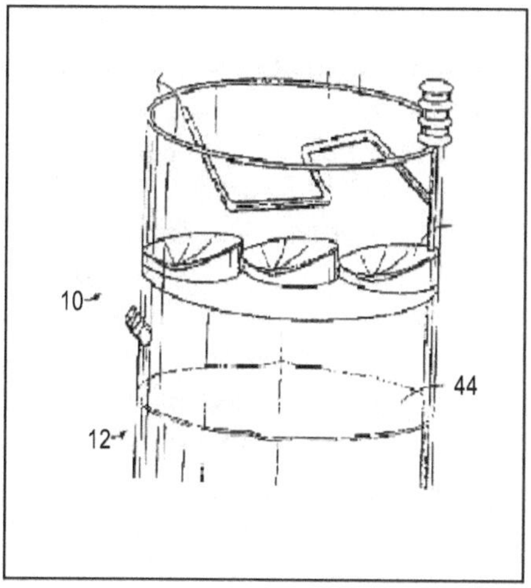

Fig. 2: Is a perspective view of the solar water heater with a plurality of parabolic reflectors.

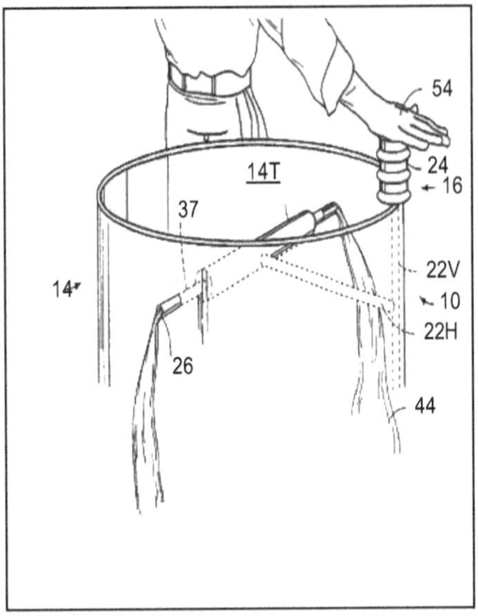

Fig. 3: Is a perspective view of a user employing the air pump to begin the flow of water.

The invention has been described as below:

Fig:1 illustrates a perspective view of the solar water heater 10 having a single stainless steel parabola 40 for collecting sunlight. The solar heater 10 comprises a cylindrical water tank 12 and a substantially cylindrical solar heating compartment 14. The water tank inlet connection 30 and a water tank drain 56, both extending fully through the side surface 12S. The water tank 12 is shown substantially filled with water 44.

The heating compartment 14 has a circular bottom surface 14B which overlaps the top surface. 12 T of the water tank, 12, and a top surface 14T and a side surface 14S which are both constructed from a transparent material such as glass or plastic. The bottom surface 14B is preferably constructed from a material which insulates against heat loss from the water tank 12. The heating compartment 14 has a substantially centrally located cylindrical copper water reservoir 24 having two flat circular end portins 24E and a surface 24S, cylindrical copper water tubing 32 extending from both end portions 24E, and two hot water outlet 26 extending from the water tubing 32 fully through the side 14S of the heating compartmet 14, whereby hot water may be released for use.

In an alternative embodiment, a single hot water outlet may be provided. The heating compartment 14 also comprises a single parabolic reflector 40 having a curved upper surface 40U, which is oriented facing upward. The parabolic reflector 40 is constructed from hightly reflective stainless steel and causes the incident rays of sunlight to be reflected and converged at a focal point of the parabola substantially upon the surface 24S of the water reservoir 24. In this regard the copper which is used for the water reservoir 24 should preferably not be highly reflective, because it is desirable that most of the light which is reflected from the parabolic reflector 40 should be absorbed by the water reservoir 24 in order to maximize the heating efficiency of the solar water heater 10.

The solar heater 20 further comprises an air pump 16, in communication with the water reservoir 24 and the water tubing 32 extending there from. The air pump 16 has air pump handel 20, vertical air pump tubing 22V, and horizontal air pump tubing 22H. The air pump 16 creates a partial vacuum in the water tubing 32, thereby causing water to flow from the water tank 12 into the water reservoir 24 and the water tubing 32. Once the siphoning of water has begur, the air-pump 16 is no longer needed to maintain a flow of water. Water ill continue to flow from the hot water outlets 26 of the solar water heater 10 until the partial vacuum is released by opening the air pump tubing to the atmosphere. In order that the flow of water from the solar water heater 10 remains uninterrupted, the hot water outlet 26 is generally connected to hose having an outlet which is maintained at a lower level than the water 44 in the water tank 12, thereby preventing the siphon from "breaking". An electric pump may be utilized instead of a manual air pump.

Fig 2 show an alternate design where the solar water heater comprises a plurality of parabolic reflectors instead of once large parabolic reflector, and instead of centrally located water reservoir 24 in fig 1 there is a convoluted stretch of water tubling. The parabolic reflectors are situated at positions which 'result'in the reflected light to converge on different portions of the surface of the tubing, in this design only one water outlet is present.

Fig 3 shows a user initiating the water flow from the water tubing 32 by creating a partial vacuum in the tube 32 by pressing and releasing the air pump handle 20, once the stream 46 has started it will continue till the tank becomes empty or the siphon effect is broken or releasing the tubing to atm pressure.

The Main components of a Patent specification are:

1. Title of the Invention
2. Field of the Invention
3. Prior Art and its drawbacks
4. Object of the invention
5. Summary of the Invention
6. Brief Description of the Invention
7. Detailed Description of the Invention

8. Claims
9. Drawings
10. Abstract

1. Title of the Invention

- It should sufficiently indicate subject matter and its specific feature.
- It should be normally within 15 words.
- It should avoid descriptive matter.
- It should be free from ambiguity.
- It should be as precise and definite.
- The followings are not allowable in the title:
    - inventor's name;
    - the word 'Patent';
    - words in other languages;
    - the abbreviation;
    - any fancy words defining properties of the invention e.g. "Washwell Soap"
- It should be Short and Simple having technical nature
- With respect to the case study: Portable Solar water Heater

2. Field of the Invention

- It should begin with a short general statement of the invention so as to show its scope and the area of technology to which it belongs to.
- It should indicate possible areas for applications and use of the invention (if it is not evident)
- With respect to the case study:
- Starts with sentence "**The present invention relates to..........**'

The present invention relates to heating apparatus and, more particularly to a solar water heater with an integrated storage tank that contributes substantially to the ecology and to saving fossil resources. This presumes well operating, rugged systems that are as passive as possible, i.e.; do not require auxiliary energy inputs.

3. Prior Art and its drawbacks

- Identify the closest prior art existing at the time of application.
- Compare your invention with prior art.
- Find out disadvantages of prior art compared to your invention.
- Highlight disadvantages or problems associated prior art.
- Extract novel features and advantages of your invention before going for a prior art search.
- Summarize the need for the invention and disadvantages of prior art.
- With respect to the case study:

"Various solar water heaters are available in the prior art but they are bulky, discomfort and not suitable for transporting.

"Patent No. XYZ discloses solar water heater with a titled, flat solar radiation absorber panel and a storage tank that performs thermo siphoning when the tank is full, whereby hot water will rise relative to cooler water. However, it contemplates heating cold water by direct absorption of solar energy, and subsequently circulating the heated water by thermo siphoning. Accordingly, ***it does not provide a solar water heater in which reflected sunlight is directed to a single location.***

Although the above described systems have assisted in solving problems present in the design of an efficient solar water heater, these arrangements still leave scope for improvement to provide a comfort and cost effective solar water heater capable of heating water user friendly and they would not be as suitable for the purposes of the present instant invention. The main disadvantage of all aforesaid inventions is that a proportion of solar energy, directly received by the absorber may have a chance to dissipate the heat energy into atmosphere due to its flat surface and for it being exposed directly to the sunlight. Another disadvantage of aforesaid inventions is they are bulky and seems to discomfort for the user."

4. Object of the Invention

- It clearly brings out the **necessity** of the invention
- It clearly indicates **advantages** of the invention.
- The following language is generally used while writing the object of the invention:
  - The main object of the invention is to provide ....
  - Another object of the invention is to provide ....
  - Still another object of the invention is ....

- A further object of the invention is ....

- Example:

*'**The main object of this invention** is to provide a solar water heater which is portable. Accordingly, the solar water heater is available in sizes which are small enough to be easily transported by an average user.*

***Another object of the present invention** is to reflect and converge the collected solar energy at the focal point upon the absorber, kept inside the heating system, to efficiently heat the water stored therein. Accordingly, a parabolic reflector is provided.*

***Still another object of this invention** is to produce a solar water heater which is energy-efficient and environmentally safe. Accordingly, the water heater is powered by solar energy and does not need electricity to operate.*

5. Summary of the invention

- The opening para should consists of most essential and distinguishing novel features of the invention.
- It should also express detail essential novel features.
- The content of the summary should list preferred and optional features (various embodiments/aspects)
- Example:

The present invention is a solar water heater comprising a water tank, a solar heating compartment for heating water, and an air pump. The water tank and the solar heating compartment are both substantially cylindrical, and the bottom surface of the heating compartment overlaps the top surface of the water tank.

The solar heating compartment has an upper surface and a side surface which are substantially constructed form transparent materials. The heating compartment contains water tubing in communication with water in the water tank and at least one stainless steel parabolic reflector positioned for reflecting incident sunlight upon the water tubing for absorption.

The water tubing terminates in at least one hot water outlet. The air pump is in communication with the water tubing within the solar heating compartment. Operation of the air pump causes a stream of water to continuously flow from the water tank to the hot water outlets by the siphoning effect.

6. Brief description of the drawings

- It is only added when there are drawings in the invention.
- The **Start of the brief description should be with the following sentence**:

"This invention is illustrated in the accompanying drawings, throughout which like reference letters indicate corresponding parts in the various figures."

- Provides a series of separate paragraphs, each briefly describing a respective view of your drawing i.e. front view, top view, isometric view, exploded view etc.
- With respect to the case study:

"Fig. 1 is perspective view of the solar water heater with a single parabolic reflector.

Fig.2 is a perspective view of the solar water heater with a plurality of parabolic reflectors.

Fig. 3 is a perspective view of a user employing the air pump to begin the flow of water."

7. Description of the invention

- Should have enough detail so that an individual with an average understanding of the field could use or reproduce the invention.
- Should disclose best method/example of working of the invention.
- Sufficient detail so as to give complete information of the invention.
- Reference to the drawings should be specific.
- Overview of the main elements of the invention and how they cooperate together.
- Hierarchical approach: Description proceeds from the more general to specific parts.
- First broad description then each element is described in detail.
- **Use of 'A' and 'The':**
    - While introducing an element **first time**, use '**a**'.

Example: *The device has* ***a handle*** *10 connected to* ***a liver*** *20*

- While referring again to something **already introduced**, use '**the**'

Example: ***The Parabola 40*** is made of stainless steel

Name for each part should be used consistently throughout the description of the invention.

- With respect to the case study:

" A solar water heater ***as illustrated in fig. 1****, has* ***a*** *stainless steel parabola (40) for collecting sunlight. The solar water heater (10) comprises* ***a*** *cylindrical water tank (12) and a substantially cylindrical solar heating compartment (14).* ***The*** *water tank (12) has a top surface (12T),* ***a*** *bottom surface (12B),* ***a*** *side surface (12S), and a water tank inlet connection (30) and* ***a*** *water tank drain (56), both extending fully through the side surface (12S).* ***The*** *water tank (12) is shown substantially filled with water (44)………*

8. Claims

- It is the crucial part or heart of the specification for protection i.e. **the only part of the invention that gets legal protection.**
- It clearly defines the boundaries and scope of the invention so that others may know the exact boundaries of the area of protection in which they should not trespass.
- It must relate to single invention and must support the description.
- It should be of **single sentence,** clear, non-redundant, succinct and not to be verbose.
- It should be expressed in **techno-legal language.**
- Claim should start from a new page.
- Claims must be supported by the description (fairly based on the description). This means that all the characteristics of the invention that form the part of the claims must be fully explained in the description
- In a claim **avoid words** like thin, strong, small, large, big, power full, it, that, they, etc.
- A claim **can be for a product, process or apparatus** and can be combination of product and process, process and apparatus but a claim having combination of all three i.e. product, process and apparatus may not be allowed in a single application based on circumstances of the case.
- A claim usually consists of three parts :
  - **Introductory phrase (preamble):** identifies the category of the invention and sometimes the purpose (For example, a machine for waxing paper, a composition for fertilizing soil).
  - **Body of the claim:** Specific legal description of the exact invention, which is sought to be protected.
  - **Link:** Joins the two segments i.e. **introductory phrase** and the **body** of the claims.The link consists of words and phrases such as :
    - Comprises

    - Including
    - Containing
    - Consisting of
    - Consisting essentially of
- Types of Claims:
    - Independent Claim
    - Dependent Claim
    - Omnibus Claim

Independent Claim

This is the first claim which is also called the **'Principal Claim'** should clearly define the essential novel features of the most preferred embodiment of the process, apparatus, device or the product.

With respect to the case study:

Portable solar water heater comprising; a water tank (12) with substantially filled water (44) having a top surface (12T), a bottom surface (12B) and at least one side surface (12S) from or through which a water tank inlet (30) and a water tank drain (56) are extending out; a solar heating compartment (14) also having a top surface (14T), a bottom surface (14B) and at least one side surface (14S); and an air pump (16);

where in said solar heating compartment (14) further comprising water tubing (24), a hot water outlet and at least one parabolic reflector (40);

where in said water tubing (24) is in communication with the water (44) in the water tank (12);

where in said hot water outlet (26) is extending from said water tubing (24);

where in the parabolic reflector (40) being positioned to reflect incident sunlight upon the water tubing (24) for absorption thereupon;

where in the solar heating compartment being atmospherically sealed.

Dependent Claim

Claims that refer to previous claims using wording such as "... as claimed in (or as defined by, or according to) claim 1 or claim 2..."

With respect to the example:

1. Portable solar water heater **as claimed in claim 1**, wherein both the water tank (12) and the solar heating compartment (14) are substantially cylindrical, wherein the bottom surface (14B) substantially overlaps the top surface (12T) and are constructed from insulator and wherein said top surface (14T) and side surface (14S) are constructed from transparent materials.
2. *Portable solar water heater* ***as claimed in claim 1****, wherein the solar heating compartment (14) optionally comprise a plurality of parabolic reflector (1) and wherein the water tubing (24) is convoluted, thereby resulting in a larger surface area of the water tubing upon which light reflected from said parabolic reflectors may be absorbed.*

Omnibus Claim

It is the last claim to get an integral protection of what is described in the specification and drawings. Now a day's these types of claims are rejected or are not used.

9. Drawing

- Drawing should be filed on a **standard A4 size** sheet in duplicate.
- Drawing should be preferably drawn in black Indian indelible ink or durable paper with margin of 2.5 cm on each side, in upright position with respect to top & bottom position of the sheet.
- Reference letter/numerals as used in the description should also be used in denoting the corresponding component/part in the figure (s).
- No descriptive matter should appear on drawings, except under certain cases, such as, **flow chart, chemical and other reaction**, etc. The **same letters or numerals** should be used in different figures for the **same parts**. In complicated drawings or when there is no room to write the reference letters in their proper places, the letters should be shown outside the figures and connected by fine lines with the parts to which they refer.

10. Abstract

- The purpose is to enable third persons to quickly determine the nature and gist of the technical disclosure while searching or studying i.e. a concise summary.
- One should understand the technical field, to which the invention belongs.
- It should be of single para having not more than 150 words.
- It must include efficient features for searching the relevant art.

- Abstract should be such that it is efficient to access whether there is any need to refer specification
- It must include relevant figure.
- Example:

The present invention discloses a portable solar water heater comprising a water tank (12), a solar heating compartment (14) for heating water, and an air pump (16). The solar heating compartment (14) has an upper surface (14T) and a side surface (14S). The heating compartment comprises a water tubing (24) in communication with water (44) in the water tank (12) and at least one stainless steel parabolic reflector (40) positioned for reflecting incident sunlight upon the water tubing (24) for absorption. The water tubing (24) terminates in at least one hot water outlet (26). The air pump (16) is in communication with the water tubing (24) within the solar heating compartment (14). Operation of the air pump (16) causes a stream of water to continuously flow from the water tank (12) to the hot water outlets (26) by the siphoning effect.

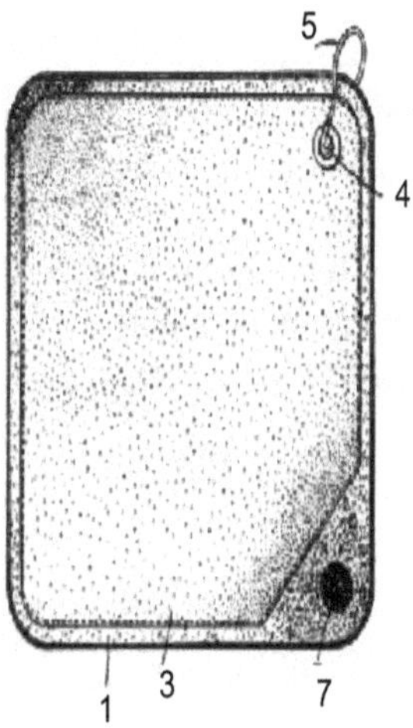

Fig 1

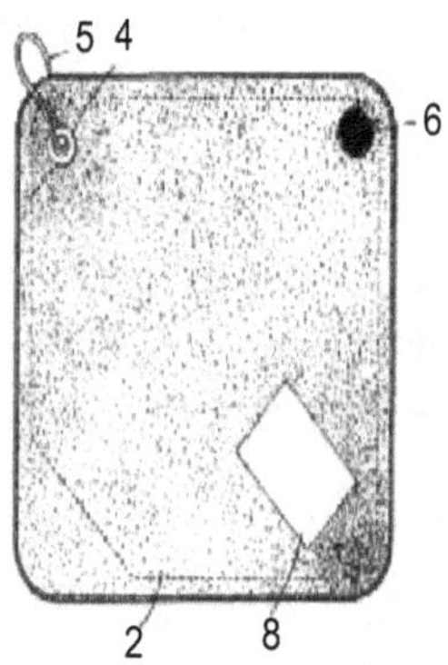

Fig 2

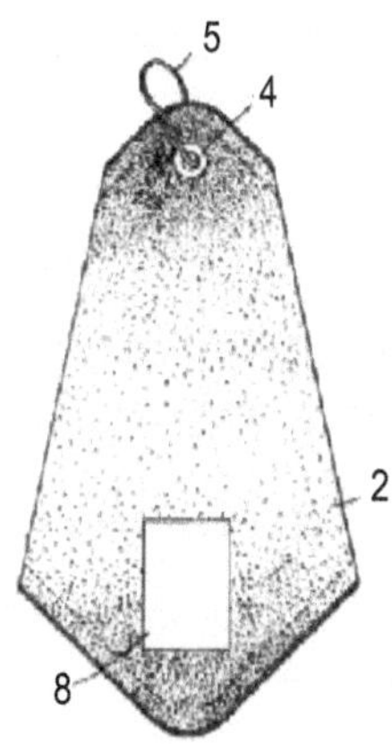

Fig 3

Title of Invention

A Gripping Aid *or* An Aid for Gripping Objects *or* Non-Slippery Gripping Aid

Field of the Invention

This invention relates to an aid for gripping objects.

The present invention more particularly **relates to** a gripping aid with a fabric impregnated with a non-slippery material attached in layer to a terry-cloth towel.

Prior art and its drawbacks

The **problem of secure gripping is present in all the sports with hand-held objects** like golf, cricket, hockey, baseball, tennis, polo, etc. Thus there is **need for a non slippery gripping** aid for every sport.

Also special implements for the secure gripping of the ball along with use of the gloves by the players and wearing helmets are widely used in all sports.

Object of the Invention

The main object of the present invention is to provide with a convenient gripping aid for hand-held athletic or sporting items.

Another object of the present invention is to provide a durable, simple and effective aid for gripping.

A further object of the present invention is an inexpensive gripping aid which can be conveniently disposed at or near the point at which it is needed.

Summary of this invention

The invention resides in a layered structure of flexible materials, one layer of which is impregnated with non-slip material and another layer so disposed as to normally enclose and cover the impregnated layer. Size of the preferred embodiments of the invention is not critical and may be adjusted to suit requirements. Quick release fasteners are employed to permit easy access to the impregnated layer and suitable hangers and engagements permit the gripping aid to be supported for hand contact and wiping.

Brief Description of the drawings

This invention is illustrated in the accompanying drawings, throughout which like reference letters indicate corresponding parts in the various figures.

Fig. 1 describes the front elevation of the invention showing the gripping aid unfolded with a hanger and a logo on the outside of the aid. (Like wise for all other drawings)

Detailed Description of the invention

In Fig. 1 and 2, a form of the invention suitable for use by a golfer is shown. It includes a layer of toweling (1) which may include a border (2). The material can be any conventional closed-loop terry cloth.

To the layer of toweling a layer of imitation chamois cloth (3) is attached by conventional sewing, heat sealing or cementing. The layer (3) is preferably somewhat smaller in area than the layer (1) to provide a degree of protection from unwanted contact with the layer (3). An opening is formed by conventional means through the dual layers adjacent a corner of the rectangular structure and a grommet (4) is fixed in the opening.

At a corner 90° removed from the corner at which the grommet (4) is inserted, the chamois layer (3) may be cut back to expose a portion of the layer (1). In that portion of the layer (1), a patch (6) of hook-and-loop material may be attached by sewing, cementing or heat sealing. The corner opposite that at which the patch (5) is attached accommodates the second matching hook-and-loop member (7). In order that the hook-and-loop members can serve to hold the toweling layer (1) in an enclosing relationship to the chamois layer (3), the second hook-and-loop member (7) is attached at the undersurface of the layer of toweling (1).

In FIG. 3, the gripping aid of the invention is shown in folded condition. It will be noted that the chamois layer (3) is so enclosed that no portion of it is exposed to the elements. Although the chamois layer (3) is so impregnated with non-slip material that it remains useful as a source of non-slip material when the hands are wiped over the layer, its usefulness is prolonged even more greatly by reason of its protective cover provided by the layer (1) folded about it.

Claims

We Claim

An aid for improving the gripping of a hand-held sporting implement comprising a generally rectangular piece of toweling (1), a similarly shaped but smaller piece of artificial chamois cloth (3) attached in underlying relationship to said piece of toweling (1), said chamois cloth (3) being impregnated with non-slip material, an opening being formed through a corner of said toweling (1), a grommet (4) disposed in said opening, a hanger (5) engaging said grommet (4), and hook-and-loop fasteners (6, 7) disposed on opposite faces of said toweling to hold the toweling (1) and chamois cloth (3) in a normally folded condition.

Exercise II [3]

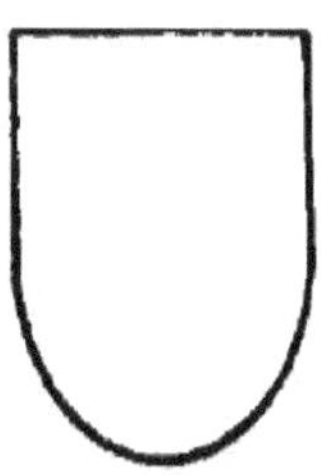

Fig 1

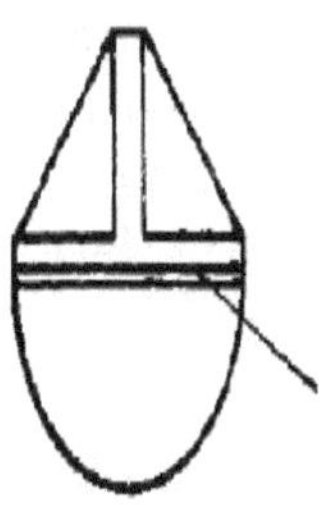

Fig 2

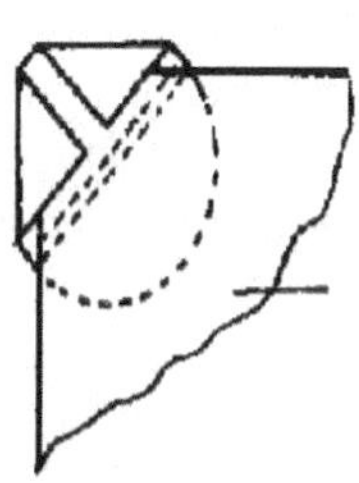

Fig 3

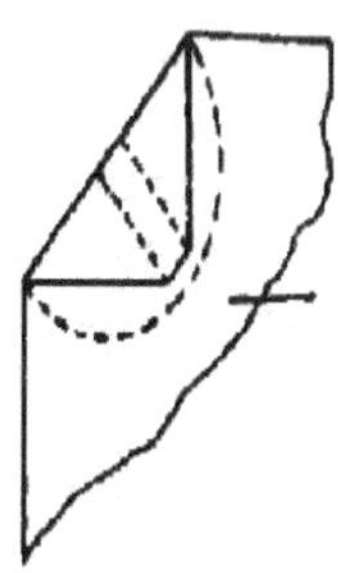

Fig 4

Title of Invention

A Paper Clip *or* A Paper Fastening Clip

Field of the Invention

This invention relates to a clip for fastening papers together for easy use.

The present invention more particularly **relates to** a metal foil or sheet employed for the fastening of paper sheets together.

Object of the Invention

The principle object of the present invention is to provide a paper clip for fastening or clipping paper sheets together in a neat way and to be able to unfasten the sheets if and when so desired.

Summary of this invention

According to this invention the device is made of thin metal sheet or foil having, originally four sides, with three of them straight and perpendicular to each other. The two corners formed by the three sides are folded down with some space left beneath them. The fourth side is left plain to have a semicircular or other shape.

Brief Description of the drawings

Fig 1 illustrates the two corners of the blank folded down with some space left beneath so that a triangular pocket is formed underneath.

Fig 2 the clip with the sheets of paper (2) inserted in the clip.

Detailed Description of the invention

As shown in Figure 1, the metal sheet or foil originally has four sides, with three of them straight and perpendicular to each other. The two corners formed by the three sides are folded down with some space left beneath them The fourth side is left plain to have a semicircular or other shape. The two corners folded down as aforesaid form a triangular pocket for the insertion of the corner of the paper sheets in the paper clip. After insertion this triangular pocket is pressed down together with the sheet corners, in order that the corners are fastened together. A crease (1) is provided below the triangular pocket to facilitate the folding down or bending of the clip and enable it to sandwich the sheets between the two halves of the clip.

The advantages of this invention is that there is no chance of the paper getting torn as may happen with conventional paper clips made of metal wires which are now in popular use. It also gives a neat appearance and there is *no* chance of anyone or more sheets coming loose due to positive grip on all the sheets (2) clipped together. The clip can also be removed by unfolding at the crease line (1) and pulling out the paper sheets from the triangular pocket. This will also be much cheaper to manufacture than the conventional paper clips made of metal wire.

Claims

We Claim:

1. A paper clip for fastening and unfastening sheet of paper together at their one corner, made of thin sheet metal or foil, having a triangular pocket formed at one end to facilitate the entry and holding of the corners of the papers-sheets together, the other end extended and formed to have a suitable shape, with a crease below the triangular pocket, to facilitate the folding down of the triangular pocket and sandwiching the paper sheets between the two halves of the clip.

Exercise III[4]

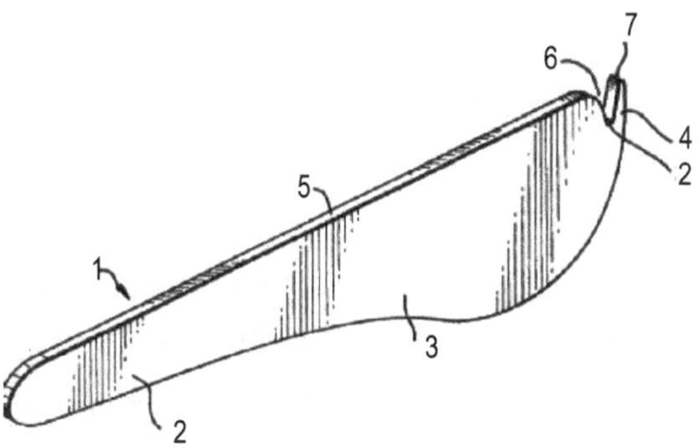

Fig 1

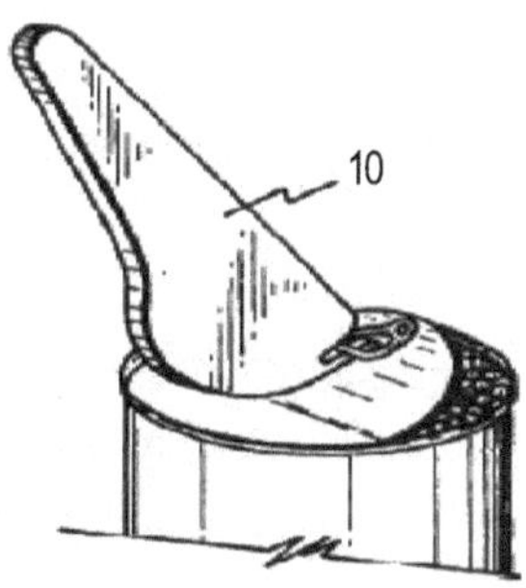

Fig 2

Title of Invention

Can Opener or Tear Top Can Opener

Field and Use of the Invention

The present invention relates to a tear top can opener, and more particularly to a can opener for use with ring-type opening tabs.

Object of the Invention

The main object of the present invention is to provide a can opener for ring-type opener tabs located at the peripheral edges of a container which aids in completely removing tear top lids from food or beverage cans.

Another object of the present invention is to provide a can opener for ring-type opener tabs which can be used by any variety of persons

Yet Another object of the present invention is to provide a can opener which is simple in structure and easy to use to completely remove "tear-off" lid can structures

Summary of this invention

The present invention is a can opener for removing the entire top from food cans where the ring-type opener tab is located adjacent the edge of the top of the can. In these types of cans, the ring-type opener is integrally attached to a removable lid portion defined by a weakened tear line around the inner periphery of the top of the can. With this structure, the ring must be engaged at the edge of the can and pulled straight up, 90 degrees to the can, in order to be able to fracture the weakened portion of the can top near the edge of the can. Once the top is initially separated, it must continue to be raised upwardly and rearward to completely remove it from the top of the can..

Brief Description of the drawings

Fig. 1 is an elevation view of the can opener of the present invention.

Detailed Description of the invention

Referring to the drawings, the can opener (1) of the present invention includes a handle end with a handle (2), an intermediate, bulbous body portion (3) and an opener end (4). The upper edge (5) of the body portion (3) of the can opener (1) is preferably straight and parallel to the longitudinal axis of the opener (1), whereas the bottom of the bulbous body portion is parabolic in shape and forms a pivoting edge along its periphery which rides on the container top during the opening process as described herein below.

The slot (6) and the finger (7) formed thereby are oriented at a 90 degree angle with respect to the longitudinal axis of the can opener (1). This is a key feature of the structure of the invention in combination with the parabolic pivoting edge.

In use, the flat outer edge of the can opener (1) is placed against the top lid of the container to be opened and the finger (7) is slid into the pull ring adjacent the peripheral edge of the container.

Once the pull ring is engaged, the can opener (1) is rotated downwardly using the parabolic pivoting edge as a fulcrum for the opener (1). The shape of the pivoting edge raises the finger (7) vertically at 90 degrees to the top of the container through the downward rotation of the handle (2) of the opener (1), thereby lifting the pull ring to sever the lid along the score line and separating the lid from the container.

It will be appreciated that continued rotation of the can opener (10) on the pivoting edge 17 will further displace the lid upwardly and rearward until it is completely removed.

Claims

We Claim:

1. A tear top can opener (1) for opening a closure lid of a container, the closure lid having a pull ring operably connected to a weakened score line, the pull ring being located adjacent the peripheral edge of the container, the opener comprising:

   a handle (2) for grasping the opener;

   an intermediate bulbous shaped body (3) portion adjacent said handle having a closure lid; and,

   an opener end adjacent intermediate portion having an end edge and a slot located adjacent end edge defining a finger (7); said finger being sized for insertion into said pull ring whereby said pull ring is held in slot during the opening operation permitting the pull ring to be lifted in a perpendicular direction to remove the closure lid.

2. The tear top can opener of claim 1 wherein said parabolic shaped pivoting edge is defined by a gradually decreasing radius toward the opener end.

3. The tear top can opener of claim 1 wherein said handle, said body portion and said opener end are integrally formed in an elongated shape.

References

1. Indian Patent Office Patent agent Examination Paper II 2008, April

2. US Patnet No. 5060943

3. IN Patent No. 135121

4. US Patent No. 5018409

6

Introduction to Patent Infringement and Defenses Against Infringement

Manish Kumar and Anil K. Pandey

Abstract

An intellectual property infringement is the violation of an intellectual property right of the owner. Infringement is established based on the law governing appropriate IPR in the concerned country. Both civil and criminal remedies are available under the concerned law. The present paper introduces the patent infringement as per Indian Patent Act, 1970. It discusses various modes and types of infringements which can take place. It further discusses a procedure to formulate opinion about product infringing a granted patent. In the end some usual defenses against patent infringements have been discussed. Some case studies have also been presented along with the damages awarded for the patent infringement.

Introduction

As per the Indian Patent Act, 1970 the rights conferred by the patentee is the exclusive right to make, use, exercise, sell or distribute the invention in India. However the 2002 amendment in the Indian Patent Act refrain the section 48 and state the patentee rights as where the subject matter of the patent is a product or process, the exclusive right to prevent third parties, who do not have his consent, from the act of making, using, offering for sale, selling or importing that product in India or product obtained directly from that process. Patent infringement refers violation of such rights. It is basically unauthorized making, using, offering for sale or selling any patented invention within territory of protection during the term of the patent. It can be termed as violation of the monopoly rights conferred to the patentee by the patent granting authority for the specified jurisdiction.

As per the Patent Act one needs to understand that one patent does not infringe another patent. Only a product or a process or an apparatus can infringe a patent, and to do so the product, process or apparatus need only infringe a single claim of the patent no matter how many claims the patent has.

There are two types of infringement

1. Literal infringement, and
2. Infringement by means of Doctrine of Equivalents

There are number of ways, in which a party can infringe a patent, including:

1. Direct infringement
2. Contributory infringement,
3. Inducing infringement, and
4. Shipping into the jurisdiction, a product which is made outside the jurisdiction in accordance with a process covered by a Patent.

Types Of Infringement

Literal Infringement

In order for a patent claim to be literally infringed

1. In case of product or apparatus claim
    - Each and every element of the claim must be found in the accused product or apparatus
2. In case of process or method claim
    - Each and every step of method or process claim must be found in the accused claim

Example

Patent granted for bearing comprises of the following claims:

1. A rolling element bearing comprising:
    a. an outer race cylindrical in shape;
    b. an inner race cylindrical in shape and concentric to said outer race and having a diameter smaller than the outer race;
    c. plurality of rolling elements contained between said outer and inner race; and
    d. means for separating each of the adjacent rolling elements.

2. The rolling element in claim 1 is a ball, wherein the said bearing acts as a ball bearing.
3. A rolling element bearing in Claim 1 wherein said bearing is an axial bearing.
4. A rolling element bearing to Claim 1 wherein said bearing is a radial bearing.
5. A rolling element bearing to Claim 1 wherein said bearing is a thrust bearing.

Some party comes up with the ball bearing as shown below and the patent holder sues the party for infringement.

Accused infringing product is a shown below:

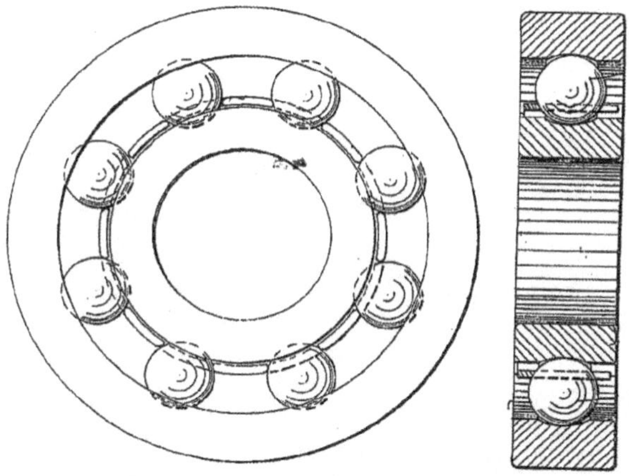

The ball bearing shown above is accused for infringing the patent granted for bearing. We need to check in light of the granted claims as mentioned above if this ball bearing literally infringe the granted patent or not?.

Starting with claim 1, it is clear that outer and inner race as recited in paragraph (a) and (b) can be found in the accused bearing. Regarding paragraph (c) it can be seen that language used is broad enough which encapsulate the balls as a rolling element and that too in plurality. In paragraph (d) it is mentioned means for separating each of the adjacent rolling elements which is done by the cage in the ball bearing.

As each element of claim 1 is reading on the accused bearing, it can be concluded that it's a case of literal infringement.

Infringement under Doctrine of Equivalents

There are two tests for determining whether an accused device or process is deemed to be equivalent. Under the first test called the "triple identity" test, something is deemed equivalent if: [3]

- It performs substantially the same function
- In substantially the same way
- To yield substantially the same result.

Under the second test, something is deemed equivalent if there is only an "insubstantial change" between each of the elements of the accused device or process and each of the elements of the patent claim. This doctrine is limited primarily by prosecution history estoppels, which prevents a claim from being made for infringement where the difference is something that the patentee abandoned through an amendment to the patent before it issued.

Modes of Infringements

There are various modes of infringing the patents. Some of the prominent modes are as follows:

Direct Infringement

A party, who makes, uses or sells in India a patented item that infringes one or more claim of a patent of another, directly infringes the patent. Similarly a party who carries out a method that infringes at least one method claim of a patent directly infringes that patent.

Contributory Infringement

If a party X furnishes a key component forming part of a combination of components to another party Y who uses it in combination with other components, and directly infringe a patent directed to the combination, then the contributing party X is guilty of contributory infringement. In this case there must be a direct infringement by Y and component furnished must be one which is not used for any different purpose but rather only or primarily as part of the patented combination.

Inducing Infringement

If Party X sells a key component to Party Y and encourages Party Y to use it in a product in a way which Party X knows will infringe the patent. Party X may be guilty of inducing infringement and this is so even if the component has other uses.

Selling a product into the protected jurisdiction from abroad

Assuming Party X has an Indian patent on a process to make a product, but no claim to the product itself. If Party Y tries to avoid infringing the patent by making the product in an otherwise infringing way in the foreign country (where X does not have a patent), and then ships the product into this country, then Party Y will be guilty of infringement.

Procedure to Formulate Opinion about Infringing Product

In order to determine if the alleged infringer is actually indulge in infringement, three questions needs to be answered:

a. The extent of monopoly right conferred by the patent which has to be ascertained by the construction of the specification and particularly the claims.

b. Whether the alleged acts amount to making , using, exercising, selling or distributing a product or using or exercising a method or process in the case of a process patent, and

c. Whether what the alleged infringer is doing amounts to an infringement of the monopoly conferred by the patent granted.

Usually claims charts are used to formulate an opinion about infringement. It is important that claim by claim, element by element analysis is done. For this claims are broken into elements and sub elements and each element and sub-element is compared with the accused product claims.

Claim Chart includes a re-writing of an independent claim so that each element of the claim is separated from the other elements for analysis purposes.

If an individual claim element is found in an accused device, a "Yes" is placed next to that element. If the individual claim element is not found in the accused device, a "No" is placed next to that element. A single "No" can defeat a charge of infringement.

Patent Claims	Accused Product /Process
Claim 1	
Element 1	
- Sub Element 1	Yes
- Sub Element 2	No
Element 2	
- Sub Element 1	Yes

Example

A company X is interested in manufacturing a Can Crushing device. A figure of the Product is given below. On the basis of the figure, analyze whether the Company X has freedom to Operate in view of Claim 1 of US 4345520.

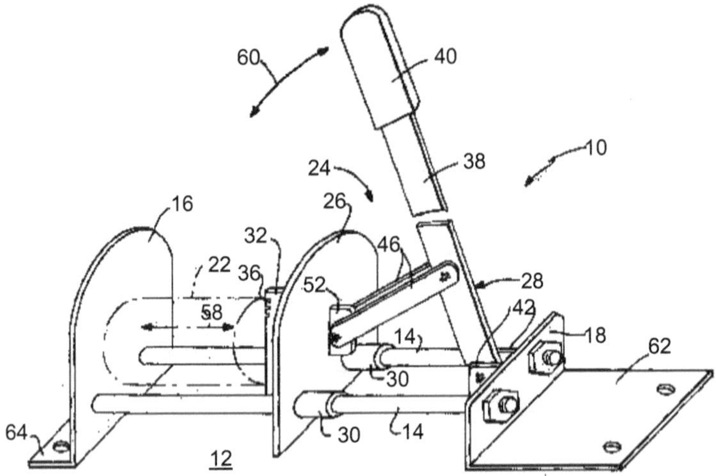

Product in Question

US Patent 4345520	Accused Product In Question
Claim 1	
1. A portable can crushing apparatus comprising:	
a. means including a pair of spacedapart parallel rods and a front end plate normal to and connected with said rods at forward most ends of the latter for supporting a can to be crushed on and extending between said rods with one end of the can resting against said front end plate;	Yes
b. a back end plate connected with and supporting rearwardmost ends of said rods;	Yes
c. can crushing means including a crush plate mounted for slidable movement along said rods in confronting relationship with said front end plate and handle means located between said crush plate and back end plate for moving said crush plate towards and away from said front end plate, whereby to crush said can; and	Yes
d. a holding plate connected to and extending rearwardly of said back end plate in a plane parallel with and below said rods so as to serve as a footrest for maintaining the end plates and rods in place as a can is crushed on a horizontal support surface.	Yes

Based on the claim chart prepared above it can be concluded that the accused product is infringing the claim 1 of the granted patent literally.

Remedies against Infringement

When Intellectual Property infringement happens, the owner may approach appropriate court for the relief. Following remedies are possible against infringement:

1. **Interim injunction:** owner of the IP at the start of a trial can request for an interim injunction to stop the defendant from continuing the acts complained of until the hearing of the action or further orders.
2. **Permanent Injunction:** Based on the merit and outcome of the case at the end of trial.
3. **Relief of Damages:** Award of damages based on the losses suffered by the claimant due to infringement of his/her IP.
4. **Account of Profits:** In this focus is on the profits made by the defendant, without taking into account the damages suffered by the claimant.

Action of Infringement

Right to sue for infringement belongs to either patentee or exclusive licensee. An action of infringement of a patent must be instituted by the way of a suit in any district court or a High Court having jurisdiction to try the suit. Where a counter-claim for revocation of the patent is made by the defendant, the suit, along with the counter-claim, shall be transferred to the High Court for decision.

The suit for infringement can be initiated only after the grant of the patent, but the damages may be claimed from the date of publication of the granted application. This period between the date of acceptance and the date of grant is termed as provisional protection. Further the suit for infringement of a patent, which has expired, may be filed to claim damages sustained during the patent tenure. Another important point to note is in the situation when a patent get lapsed for whatever reason and later restored, no suit can be filed for any infringement committed between the date when patent was ceased and the date of publication of application for restoration.

Some Defenses against Infringement

The defendant in an infringement suit may plea for any of the following defenses:

- Denial of infringement
- Invalidation of claims of the granted patent, alleged to be infringed
- Estoppels
- Plaintiff not entitled to sue for infringement.
- The act is in accordance with section 47 of the Indian Patent Act, 1970(Government use, experimentation, research and education)

Some acts not considered as Infringement

As per Section 107A of The Indian Patent Act, 1970, following acts are not considered as infringement:

- Act of making, constructing, using, selling or importing a patented invention solely for uses reasonably related to the development and submission of information required under any law for the time being in force, in India, or in a country other than India, that regulates the manufacture, construction, use, sale or import of any product.
- As per Indian Patent Act, one has provisions to manufacture generic drugs by using the patented inventions for development and submission of information required under law–for example- from public health authorities-without the patent owner's permission and before the patent protection expires. The generic producers can then market their version as soon as the patent expires. This provision is called "Bolar-like provision" or "regulatory exception".
- Importation of patented products by any person from a person who is duly authorized under the law to produce and sell or distribute the product, shall not be considered as a infringement of patent rights. Hence Parallel imports are allowed. Therefore it is possible to import the patented products from the licensee of the patentee in any country with out the permission of the Patentee. The purpose of Parallel import is to check the abuse of patent rights and meant to control the price of patented product.

Some Case Studies of Patent Infringement

Samsung Electronics Settled Patent Infringement Litigation with Rambus by paying $200 Million

January 21, 2010 - Samsung Electronics Co. and Rambus, Inc. settled all patent litigation between the two companies. The patents under which Samsung have taken a license cover for all of Samsung's semiconductor products. Under the terms of the agreement, Samsung paid $200 million to Rambus, plus buy $200 million of Rambus' shares and make $25 million quarterly royalty payments to the memory-chip designer for the next five years under a patent license.

Medtronic Awarded $101 Million in Patent Infringement Lawsuit

September 21, 2011 - One of the largest jury awards in the US was handed to Medtronic Inc. in its patent lawsuit against rival NuVasive. A jury awarded Medtronic $101 million, which may go higher since it only covers damages through the summer of 2010. The patents that the jury found NuVasive infringed are owned by Warsaw Orthopedic Inc., a unit of Medtronic, and cover spine devices. The jury also found that Medtronic infringed one of NuVasive's patents and awarded NuVasive $600,000 in damages.

Some of the damage awards settled by the US court for patent infringements

Years	Jury/Bench	Plaintiff	Defendant	District Award	Appeals Decision
1990	Bench	Polaroid Crop	Eastman Kodak Co.	$909,457,567	N/A
1994	Jury	Alpex Computer Corp.	Nintendo Company Ltd.	$253,641,445	Reversed
1996	Bench	Haworth, Inc.	Steelcase Inc.	$211,499,731	N/A
1997	Bench	The Proctor & Gamble Co.	Paragon Trade Brands, Inc	$211,499, 731	N/A
1998	Bench	Exxaom Corp. & Exxon Chemical Patents Inc.	Mobil Oil Corp. & Mobil Chemical Co. Inc.	$171,000,000	N/A
1999	Bench	Hughes Aircraft Company	The Union States	$153,775,000	(a)
1994	Jury	Exxom Chemical Patents Inc.	Lubrizol Corp.	$128, 4000,000	Reversed
1994	Jury	Stac Electronics Crop.	Microsoft Corp.	$120,000,000	N/A
1991	Bench	Minnesota Mining & Manufacturing Co.	Johnson & Johnson Orthopaedics, Inc	$116, 797, 696	Affirmed
1996	Bench	Dow Chemical Co.	The United States	$86,817,461	Remuled

(a) Hughes V. The United state was appealed to the supreme Court. The court of Appeals for the Federal Circuit affirmed the decision for a second time in 1998. The Court of Federal Claims reissued the award in 1999.

Some of the damage awards settled by the US court for patent infringements

Commercial Significance of IP Protection

In 1979, Xerox in their Palo Alto Research Center developed the first GUI. They used it on their first commercial home PC, the Xerox Star, but that didn't sell very well. While the history is a bit muddled, Apple definitely knew of the work, and was influenced by the Xerox GUI when they launched the Apple Lisa and then the Mac, both with nicely working GUIs. Microsoft was late to the GUI party with Windows, but we all know where the money ended up. Mistake done by Xerox was they decided against filing a patent for this invention. Had they filed a patent for the same they might have earned almost half million dollar even at a nominal licensing fee of 1% of sales

Conclusion

In the present Socio-economic scenario of India, it has been seen that awareness about protection of Intellectual Property is increasing day by day. It becomes essential for entrepreneur, industrialist as well as academician to know about IPR infringement and repercussions of infringement. The paper introduces the patent infringement along with modes and types of infringement which may occur. It discusses some defenses and remedies against infringement along with some case studies showing damage awarded in case of some patent infringement cases. It can be concluded that in the present scenario one need to be extra vigilant to avoid any kind of IPR infringement.

References

1. The Patent Act, 1970
2. Shear, S."The Handbook on Patents and the Patent Process Volume 1", 15th Edition, (2007) Silicon Vally Seminars, Inc, USA
3. Shear, S."The Handbook on Advanced Patents and the Patent Process Volume 1", 3rd Edition, (2007) Silicon Vally Seminars, Inc, USA
4. Narayanan, P. "Intellectual Property Law" Third Edition, (2012) Eastern Law House, New Delhi.
5. Draft Manual of Patent Practice and Procedure the Patent Office, India, 2008
6. http://www.ip-holdings.com/patent-infringement-lawsuit-settlements-news
7. William, O,. Kerr, W.O., and Prakash, G, (2003) "Patent Damages And Royalty Awards:The Convergence Of Economics And Law" les Nouvelles, pp 83-91.
8. http://timkastelle.org/blog/2010/06/innovating-without-intellectual-property-protection/

7

Are All Subject Matters Patentable?

Manish Kumar and Anil K. Pandey

Abstract

The paper discusses patentability aspect of subject matter. Patentable subject matter must satisfy three basic criteria i.e. novelty, inventiveness and industrial applicability, though few subject matter satisfying all the three basic criteria stated above may still be not patentable in specific jurisdiction based on certain circumstances or as stated in the patent act of the specified jurisdiction. Therefore grant of a patent is subject to certain limitations mentioned in the section 3 and 4 of the Indian Patent Act for Indian jurisdiction. The aim of this paper is to study such limitations in detail.

Keyword: Subject matter, Invention, Patenting, Indian Patent Law, TRIPS, USPTO, EPC

Introduction

Property which can be owned can be either tangible or intangible in nature. This paper focuses only on the intangible property. Intellectual Property is used to describe the property that is intangible in nature, originating through the creative effort of the inventor. Creation of Intellectual property requires human skill, intelligence, labour and efforts as inputs. In today knowledge era, people realizes the value of the intangible products generated out of human's intellect; therefore they intend to prevent unauthorized use of such intellectual property with proper IP rights and to avail maximum commercial benefit from it.

All subject matters are not patentable. Broadly, the subject matter that satisfies the three basic criteria such as novelty, inventive step and industrial applicability is considered as patentable subject matter, though it has been defined differently in different jurisdiction.

As per section 101 of US Patent Law, the patentable subject matter has been defined as: 'whoever invents or discovers any new and useful process, machine, manufacture, or composition of matter, or any new and useful improvement thereof, may obtain a patent therefor, subject to the conditions and requirements of this title'[1]

Similarly article 2(1) of Japan Patent Law define the subject matter that can be patented is 'a highly advance creation of technical idea utilizing a law of nature' [2]. In distinct to US and Japanese patent laws, the European Patent Convention does not expressly state which sorts of inventions are patentable. However the convention illustrated the patentable subject matter or patent eligibility in opposite sense by excluding the following categories of inventions from patent, namely:

1. Discoveries, scientific theories and mathematical methods
2. Aesthetic creations
3. Schemes, rules and methods for performing mental acts, playing games or doing business and programs for computers.
4. The presentation of information [3]

As per article 27 of TRIPS agreement, the broadly definition of patentable subject matter is

Creation in any field of technology, whether products or processes are eligible for patent, if they satisfy three basic criteria such as novelty, inventiveness and industrial applicability.

However TRIPS agreement stated that member states may not allow patent to such type of invention within their territory which is necessary to protect the public order or morality, including protection of human, animal, and plant life or health or to avoid serious prejudice to the environment, provided that such exclusion is not made merely because the exploitation is prohibited by their law.

TRIPS further state that member states may also exclude from patentability:

a. diagnostic, therapeutic and surgical methods for the treatment of humans or animals;
b. plants and animals other than micro-organisms, and essentially biological processes for the production of plants or animals other than non-biological and microbiological processes. However, Members shall provide for the protection of plant varieties either by patents or by an effective sui generis system or by any combination thereof.

The provisions of this subparagraph were reviewed four years after the date of entry into force of the WTO Agreement"[4]. The Indian Patent Act corresponds to the European Convention follow negative method of excluding the categories of inventions that are not patent eligible. Thus what forms patentable subject matter in India is decided by a non-exhaustive list of things which shall not be regarded as patentable subject matter [5].

Thus, patentable subject matter or patent-eligible subject matter is a subject matter, which is susceptible of patent protection. The laws or patent practices of many countries provide that certain subject-matter is excluded from patentability, even if the invention is novel, non-obvious and having utility or industrial applicability. Therefore the question of whether a particular subject matter is patentable or not is a matter of policy and depend upon national as well as international legislation[6].

In this context, The World Trade Organization's Agreement on Trade Related Aspects of Intellectual Property Rights (the TRIPS Agreement) sets out minimum standards of intellectual property (IP) protection that member states must provide. The TRIPS Agreement describes the objectives of the intellectual property system as follows: The protection and enforcement of intellectual property rights should contribute to the promotion of technological innovation and to the transfer and dissemination of technology, to the mutual advantage of producers and users of technological knowledge and in a manner conducive to social and economic welfare, and to a balance of rights and obligations [7].

The TRIPS Agreement recognises that there are both economic and non-economic aspects to the intellectual property system. It also recognises that there needs to be an appropriate balance between the interests of patent holder and public. The TRIPS Agreement sets a general principle in favour of patentability for inventions with separate provisions for exclusion of certain subject matter on policy grounds. The objectives clauses contained in the intellectual property legislation of various nations reflect these TRIPS Agreement Principles. India being a signatory member of TRIPS agreement must need to compliance with TRIPS objectives, principles and guidelines. Also any legislation has social context and patent law is not an exception.

Thus under Indian patent legislation, the current test of patentable subject matters are decided by considering list of subject matter; which are not be regarded as patentable subject matter mentioned in the section 3 and 4 of Indian Patent Act, 1970, as amended time to time. The purpose of inserting such limitations in the Indian Patent Act is to strike a balance between public good and rights of patent holder. Therefore, if a subject matter broadly satisfy the tests of new or novelty and include an inventive step and be capable of industrial application and seems to be eligible to get patent but may not be granted patent, if it cause adverse effect on the society.

Three Corners Test for Golden Traingular Patentable Subject Matter

Among all types of IP rights, the patent right is most stringent, rigorous and involves a complex process, because patent law states that invention must need to be new, having inventive step and capable of industrial applicable to get a patent. The philosophy behind putting three corner tests for patentable is to avoid duplication in research and development activities and adopt fair trade practice.

i. Corner Test

New or Novel: An invention is said to be new if it cannot be anticipated by publication in any document or used in the country or elsewhere in the world or used in the country or prior claimed in an application for patent in India or form part of knowledge, oral or otherwise, available within any local or indigenous community in India or elsewhere before the date of filing of patent application or date of priority i.e. the subject matter has not been in public domain nor does it form the state of art(See S. 2 (1) (l) of the Indian Patent Act, 1970)[8] The phrase "state of art" though not defined in Indian Patent Act, but it can be interpreted resorting to English Law.

"The state of art in case of an invention shall be taken to comprise all matter (whether a product, a process, information about either, or anything else) which has at any time before the priority date of that invention been made available to the public (anywhere in the world) by written, oral description, use or in any other way."[9]. Such limitation of prior art is imposed on patentable subject matter to ensure that patent granting does not block people from doing what they were doing before the grant of the patent[10].

ii. Corner Test

Inventive Step or Non-Obvious: The second corner test of patentable subject matter is that the subject matter must technically be advanced as compared to existing knowledge or having economic significance or both and that makes the invention not obvious to a person skilled in art (See S. 2(1) (ja), Indian Patent Act, 1970)[8]. It means the invention should not be obvious to a person skilled in art by the way of technology or commercial point of view or both. The philosophy behind obviousness can be drawn from the landmark case of *Biswanath Prasad Radhey Shyam vs Hindustan Metal Industries, 13 December, 1978[11]* that the general public should not be prevented from doing anything, which was merely an obvious extension or workshop variation of what was already known on/ before the priority date of the patent application.

It is important to note that there is no specific testing parameter to define novelty and inventive step. The definition and standard of novelty and non-obviousness is varying from country to country and time to time. For example some country follows absolute novelty criteria to define novelty; however some country follows relative and some are mixed.

iii. Corner Test

Industrial Applicability: The third and last corner test for patentable subject matter is invention must have industrial applicability or utility.

Apart from above three basic criteria to decide patentability aspect of subject matter, various countries have adopted different approaches to define the field of patentable subject matter. Most countries provide a definition of 'invention' – either by a positive definition of invention or negatively by way of a list of subject matters that are not patentable inventions. India also put such limitations and which are illustrated in section 3 and 4 of the Indian Patent Act.

Inventions not Patentable [Sections 3 and 4 of The Indian patent Act, 1970]

Following inventions are not patentable

Frivolous Inventions and Inventions against Natural Laws

An invention which is frivolous or which claims anything obviously contrary to well-established natural laws (See S.3(a), Indian Patent Act, 1970) [8]

For example
Perpetual motion machine - A machine intended to produce perpetual motion.

The above invention is not patentable as it is claiming to give output without any input and which is against the established natural law.

Simply compilation of already existing articles without any substantial changes or interconnection is known as frivolous invention. Such as hat and torch light are well known article; therefore an invention which claims a torch light attached with hat would be considered as frivolous invention [12].

Inventions Contrary to Public Order or Morality or Prejudicial to Living Organisms or Environment

An invention the primary or intended use or commercial exploitation of which would be contrary to law or morality or which causes serious prejudice to human, animal or plant life or health or to the environment (See S.3(b), Indian Patent Act, 1970) [8]

For examples

Method of hacking into email accounts; machine for polluting air; A gambling machine [13];

None of the above inventions are patentable as they are against morality.

Scientific Principle or Abstract Theory or Discovery

The mere discovery of a scientific principle or the formulation of an abstract theory [or discovery of any living thing or non-living substance occurring in nature](See S.3(c), Indian Patent Act, 1970)[8].

For examples

Einstein theory of E = mc2, Boyle's and Charles's Law are scientific theory or principle that cannot be patented. However practical application of theory or principle to a process or product would be patentable [12]. Similarly Discovery of any living or non living occurring in nature is also not patentable. For example, discovery of plant in coastal region, which bears both watermelon and orange.

New Form or New Property or New Use of Known Substance

The mere discovery of any new form of a known substance which does not result in the enhancement of the known efficacy of that substance or mere discovery of any new property or new use for a known substance or of the mere use of a known process, machine or apparatus unless such process results in a new product or employs at least one new reactant.

Salts, esters, ethers, polymorphs, metabolites, pure forms, particle size, isomers, mixtures of isomers, complexes and combination and other derivatives of known substances will be considered as same substance and are not patentable; unless they differ significantly in properties with regard to efficacy(See S.3(d), Indian Patent Act, 1970)[8].

The efficacy needs to be shown by showing improved effect in comparison with the original substance through objective scientific evidence.

For Example

If existence of aluminium in sulphate form is well known, coming of it with a chloride form would not merit to get patent, unless aluminium in chloride form has improved effect when compared to the sulphate form.

Similarly discovery of the use of Aspirin for treating cardiovascular disease would not be patentable, if t was already using for analgesic purpose.

Mere Admixture

A substance obtained by a mere admixture resulting only in the aggregation of the properties of the components thereof or a process for producing such substance (See S.3 (e), Indian Patent Act, 1970)[8].

For examples

Mixture of sugar and colorants in water, which only produces aggregation of properties, is not patentable but admixture produces a synergistic effect of the properties of the components is patentable [13].

Admixture of diclofenac and paracetamol to cure pain and fever would not be patentable, because it is an admixture in which diclofenac and paracetamol are aggregated and work independently on pain and fever. However if above admixture produce better therapeutic benefit such as no or less side effects as compare to existing drug or quick effect or prolong effect etc.

Mere Arrangement or Re-arrangement of Devices

The mere arrangement or re-arrangement or duplication of known devices each functioning independently of one another in a known way(See S.3(f), Indian Patent Act, 1970)[8].

For example

A known type of torch connected to a know type of pen and having separate switching system is not patentable; because both the pen and torch work independently of each other. However, if the torch comes on and focuses on the paper when the nib of pen touches the paper, it would be patentable subject matter, as both systems are interdependent.[23]

Method of Agriculture or Horticulture

A method of agriculture or horticulture(See S.3(h), Indian Patent Act, 1970) [8].

For example

A method of growing plants

Medical and Surgical Methods

Any process for the medicinal, surgical, curative, prophylactic diagnostic, therapeutic or other treatment of human beings or any process for a similar treatment of animals to render them free of disease or to increase their economic value or that of their products (See S.3 (i), Indian Patent Act, 1970)[8].

For example

Process of carrying out a surgery is not a patentable subject matter. However, systems and apparatuses are still considered as patentable subject matter.

Similarly a method of whitening teeth or a method of implanting hair would be not patentable [12], but the device and system used for such process would be patentable subject matter.

Plants and Animals

Plants and animals in whole or any part thereof other than micro-organisms but including seeds, varieties and species and essentially biological processes for production or propagation of plants and animals(See S.3(j), Indian Patent Act, 1970)[8]

For example

Cloning of animals and genetically modified mouse is not patentable as it is animal.

A new variety of mango is not patentable, as it is plant

Mathematical or Business Calculations and Computer Programs

A mathematical or business method or a computer program per se or algorithms (See S.3(k), Indian Patent Act, 1970)[8].

For example

The "computer program per se" is not patentable. However, if computer program is embedded in hardware or produce a technical effect would be patentable. Like a computer program for word processing or calculation on a general purpose would not be patentable, but computer program for printing document by using printer may be patentable because its produce a technical effects. Similarly software to send message from one mobile to another mobile may be patentable, as it is embedded software [12].

Copyright and Related Rights works

A literary, dramatic, musical or artistic work or any other aesthetic creation whatsoever including cinematographic works and television productions (See S.3(l), Indian Patent Act, 1970) [8].

For example

Movies, poems etc. are not patentable, in fact they are protected under copyright and other related law

Mental Act or Method of Playing a Game

A mere scheme or rule or method of performing mental act or method of playing game (See S.3 (m), Indian Patent Act, 1970)[8].

For example

Method of playing chess is not patentable under the above stated clause.

Presentations

A presentation of information (See S.3 (n), Indian Patent Act, 1970)[8].

For example

Presenting the information in the form of a graph is not patentable under the above clause.

Integrated Circuits

Topography of integrated circuits (See S.3 (o), Indian Patent Act, 1970)[8]. It can be protected under Semiconductor Integrated Circuit Lay-out Designs Act [14].

Traditional Knowledge

An invention which in effect, is traditional knowledge or which is an aggregation or duplication of known properties of traditionally known component or components(See S.3(p), Indian Patent Act, 1970)[8].

For example

Usage of Nilgiri oil for reducing aches is not patentable as it is a traditional knowledge and which is not patentable under the above clause.

Atomic Energy

An invention related to atomic energy is not patentable. The reason for excluding such type of invention from patentable subject matter is of national security purpose.

It can be seen that there is no straight forward method to check patentability of the subject matter. Though broadly the criterion to check patentability of subject matter more or less remains same in various jurisdictions, but it has been defined differently in different jurisdiction. Some jurisdictions have defined it in a positive manner (what all is patentable) where as others have defined it in negative manner (what all is not patentable). Thus it remains a very important topic of study and needs through understanding the patent law of various jurisdictions.

Conclusion

Despite of various shortcomings in current patenting system, the patenting system is utmost important. Every subject matter is not patentable. Patentable subject matter broadly needs to satisfy the tests of new or novelty and include an inventive step and be capable of industrial application. Once it satisfied these tests then certain limitations checklists need to be imposed on patentable subject matter to balance the relationship between public good and rights of patent holder. Thus even if a subject matter qualifies for patent grant i.e. is patent eligible, it may not be granted patent if public good falls short against rights of patent holder. This paper highlights the patentability criteria for subject matter in various jurisdiction with particular emphasis on Indian Jurisdiction.

Refeences

1. http://www.uspto.gov/web/offices/pac/mpep/documents/appxl_35_U_S_C_101.htm AND United States Code
2. http://www.jpo.go.jp/tetuzuki_e/t_tokkyo_e/Guidelines/2_1.pdf AND Japan Patent Law

3. European Patent Convention, 1973, Article 52; http://www.epo.org/law-practice/legal-texts/html/epc/1973/e/ar52.html
4. http://www.wto.org/english/tratop_e/trips_e/t_agm3c_e.htm#5
5. Patentable Subject Matter and he Necessity of Limitations on it (http://papers.ssrn.com/sol3/papers.cfm?abstract_id=1981650).
6. http://www.acip.gov.au/library/Patentable%20Subject%20Matter%20Issues%20Paper.pdf
7. http://www.wto.org/english/tratop_e/trips_e/intel2_e.htm.
8. The Indian Patent Act, 1970.
9. S. 2(2) of the British Patent Act , 1977.
10.N.S. Gopala Krishnan & T.G. Agitha , Principles of Intellectual Property , Eastern Book Company, 1st edition, 2009, p.62.
11. http://indiankanoon.org/doc/1905157/
12. Kalyan C. Kankanala & et.al. , Indian Patent Law and Practice, Oxford University Press, 1st edition, 2010, p.18.
13. Draft Manual of Patent Practice and Procedure the Patent Office, India, 2008.
14. www.inventree.com.

8

Hopes and Prospects on Intellectual Properties of Grass Root Innovators under Technopreneur Promotion Programme

P.K. Ghosh

Introduction

In the perspective of the accelerating national growth rate of 8% recorded at the end of the 10th Plan to a projected growth rate of 10% by the end of the 11th Plan, yielding an average GDP growth rate of about 9% it was appearing that the nation is going to have a strong footing of development. However, it could not be fully achieved due to several reasons including the global recession and other factors related to international economic setback which may deter achieving a projected growth rate of 10% in the 12th Plan. In consideration of the international scenario of growing complicacy in economic growth more emphasis should be given on further efficient utilization of natural resources and intellectual properties of grass root innovators to improve per capita income leading to a promising national structure of economics ensuring wide spread benefits to the society. In this regard, true development of a nation like India can be primarily realized by recognition of wide spread enthusiasm of its innovative human resources living in village and rural areas. It can be made possible only through working with them by appreciating their struggle for survival using all round innovative measures coming out of their daily life experiences and traditional knowledge. Technopreneur Promotion Programme (TePP) is a unique scheme of Government of India for development of society especially by promoting the intellectual properties of grass-root level innovators coming out from the society with a source of inspiration arising out of their daily life struggle for existence. In spite of its limited publicity in remote areas an awareness of this programme has often been found to raise great hope to the villagers to do something for their society exploring the ideas generated from the experiences of life with the help of local resources. Such naturally grown innovation can be found undoubtedly novel and the idea can change their world of dreaming for a more prosperous life by bringing changes in socioeconomic pattern of trade and employment in rural areas with proper support from Government if India through the scheme like TePP.

Basic Outlook of TePP Programme

On the background of current scenario of enormous unusual changes in national economic growth in the perspective of international financial crisis the TePP can play a more positive role to support the national growth by promoting technopreneurship on intellectual properties of grass root level innovation with a more liberal and adaptive concept. This is especially true in the context of international treaties and agreements of trade and commerce. At this juncture TePP should adjudge the innovation primarily with an attitude to support the society for improvement of its regional or zonal socioeconomic quality of life especially in rural and remote areas. This is essentially to be done with a mind set to handle new concept of application often evolves out of daily life experiences without going into judging its novelty in the context of patentability or other wide scale commercial value analysis. In fact such new concepts and ideas can mostly be found innovative for the development of society, at least with regional or local perspective, by giving proper attention to it with necessary counseling. Several measures are required to deliver the results of this effort by creating an environment for generation of wealth and self employment in the society. In this regard it may be remembered that relatively poorly educated young people is having more entrepreneurial attitude for survival than a highly educated young but, their venture is mostly restricted due to non availability of required funds or credit to start a new enterprise especially on innovative technologies emerging from the rural areas. It requires harnessing the entrepreneurial abilities and skills of these people by providing avenues for self employment. Though the GoI has promoted several schemes to promote entrepreneurship, TePP is a notable scheme available for promoting technopreneurship among not only the pool of highly skilled and technically qualified professionals / students but also amongst the grass-root level individuals, for developing their ideas up to a final level of commercialization.

Hopes and Prospects of Innovators

In the perspective of the struggle for survival of the peoples from rural areas, which is a substantial part of population of our country, we have to give due consideration to their generic hopes in order to bring prospects in their life through the TePP scheme. In this regard an area that needs immediate attention is the promotion of self employment in rural areas. Large number of innovation comes up from rural areas as a mode of survival emerging out of the experiences from life of the grass-root innovators. They help not only to enhance their abilities to generate a livelihood but also serve as a useful conduit to evolve solutions for other neighbouring villages/areas having the similar problems. In this matter, often the Traditional Knowledge (TK) plays significant role, which is integral part of the cultural identity of various social groups where it operates and is preserved. The growing sufferings from various unusual developments of life turns the mind of society towards search of means to survive on the basis of solutions offered by traditional knowledge with necessary modifications, by maintaining its basic unanimity to natural resources. Many traditional habits and skills are environmentally safe and highly effective from the point of view of economy, natural energy utilization and balancing of ecosystem.

The TePP can be an efficient Government sponsored scheme to cater the hopes of the innovators from rural and remote areas by addressing their funding/ credit needs. Largely successful mission of TePP has emerged out as a scheme to encourage the common people to start a technopreneurial venture, which is in concurrence with the national policies and planning for projected economic growth of our country. Now the time has come to analyze its services that so far provided to various sections of our population. We have to be more concern to check the success of this programme in delivering its benefits to the people from rural and remote areas.

Reminiscent Measures

In consideration of all these facts it is necessary to run this programme with certain duly felt modification in its operational aspects to make it more popular and attractive to cater the hopes of innovators from rural areas. In order to do so more effectively the TePP scheme is to operate primarily for development of society by generating self employment and creating scope for local employment supporting the grass root innovators. Here the technoprenourship on innovative ideas, often by using the local resources of knowledge, experiences and raw materials, has to be encouraged based on regional or local needs and benefits rather to consider them in the perspective of wide scale commercial prospect. It requires more outreach programmes in rural and remote areas to, encourage the grass root innovators to come forward with their proposal, to cater their hopes/ expectations through appropriate counseling and technical support and to make them aware of the prospect of involvement with this scheme. The proposals from such innovators should be reviewed for funding by a committee of experts, where a substantial representation of well experienced local persons having good knowledge of strengths and weaknesses of the region is kept to consider the hopes and prospects of the innovators appropriately. The funding and operating procedure of a project should be more simplified by involvement of local authority to eliminate the fear in mind of the innovators about taking support etc. from a government body. More frequent close look system of reviewing the utilization of grant and progress of the project must be operative. More showcasing of successful projects should be planned through the media that freely operating in remote areas to encourage more people to come forward to get their dream in reality of better life with the support from TePP scheme.

9

Managing Intellectual Property Rights

Poornima Ganesh

"Necessity is the mother of invention", all of us must have heard this statement at some juncture in our lives. Most of us may even have even gone through the motion of inventing something when needed. However, more and more inventions happening today may not necessarily be necessities. These inventions definitely perform the task of improvingand making convenient our overall living environment. Past few years have seen an increasing awareness and understanding in the field of intellectual property. Among all aspects, one aspect of intellectual property that is gaining increasing attention of intellectual property owners is management of the intellectual property rights.

This brings to our minds one question, how was intellectual property management practised by early mankind? We all do know that early mankind has left no stone unturned to make theabove statement"Necessity is the mother of invention", a reality. Mankind prospered by leaps and bounds on account of sharing their various discoveries and inventions. Way back then knowledge was meant to be shared, as aptly captured in the Sanskrit Sloka:

नचोरहार्यम्नचराजहार्यम्नभ्रातृभाज्यम्नचभारकारि।
व्ययेकृतेवर्धतएवनित्यम्विद्याधनम्सर्वधनप्रदानम्॥

Meaning: The treasure that cannot berobbed by thieves, nor could be taxed by the government. It cannotbe divided among siblings nor is it a heavy load to carry. Unlike othertreasures, this one grows when you spend it! Thus knowledge or Vidya is the most important treasure that one could ever possess.

What has changed between then and now? Why there a need being felt and exercised of protecting our intellectual property rights? Why then is the discussion on intellectual property management interesting and worth focussing on?

Before going any deeper we also need to understand how a intellectual property professional differentiates between the terms: an idea, an invention, an innovation, an intellectual property and an intellectual property right. An idea can occur to anybody, it may provide a solution to a problem at hand, i.e., an idea when born is an intellectual property. An idea can be called an invention if a determination is made that statutorily the idea is novel and inventive. An inventioncan be hence be protected as an intellectual property right. An invention can be called an innovation if the idea is successful in becoming a commercial venture. It is not necessary that an innovation/invention has to be protected as an intellectual property right, it is left to the discretion of the owner. A protected intellectual property right has more weightage in a court of law in cases of infringement than an unprotected intellectual property right.

It appears that earlier methods of protecting intellectual property revolved around keeping the idea a secret. For example, let us consider the textile industry. We have often heard it mentioned that a particular dyestuff and a particular print pattern were used only for a particular fabric. So it was relatively easy not only for the manufacturer to detect infringement of their fabric, but also for the customer to buy the correct fabric of his choice. If the manufacturer kept the dyestuff used as secret, methods used then were not very helpful in reverse engineering and identifying the dyestuff. However today with the variety of fabrics and dyestuff's available and the number of permutations and combinations possible, it is practically impossible for the customer to distinguish between the fabrics. It could possibly mean that the environment of yesteryears was more conducive to secrets since secrets could be better kept, as copying and hence infringing products had their own technical difficulties. However, with the improvement in technology and increase in the knowledge base copying has become easier. Further, with the increase in the number of ideas and with the increased conversion of these ideas to intellectual property rightsin any and every field including essential fields like pharmaceuticals and healthcare, energy and power, communications, and others, known method of intellectual property management may have to be revisited.

Knowledge today is viewed not only as a necessary ingredient of a successful business but as an asset on its own. Knowledge may also be viewed as a range of strategies and practices used in an organization to identify, create, represent, distribute, and enable adoption of insights and experiences. Such insights and experiences comprise knowledge, either embodied in individuals or embedded in organizations as processes or practices. The increasing demand for knowledge in the form of ideas that may prove to be inventions and may later be transformed to workable innovations puts a burden on the knowledge industry and knowledge economy and again makes us realize that a change in the traditional management methods of intellectual property based assets like innovation and know-how is the need of the hour.

Intellectual property is a term referring to a number of distinct types of creations of the mind for which a set of exclusive rights are recognized under the corresponding fields of law. Although many of the legal principles governing intellectual property have evolved over centuries, it was not until the 19th century that the term intellectual property began to be used, and not until the late 20th century that it became commonplace in the majority of the world. The British Statute of Anne 1710 and the Statute of Monopolies 1623 are now seen as the origins of copyright and patent law respectively.

Intellectual property management is not a one-step formula that one follows to secure their intellectual property. In a first step intellectual property management includes recognizing an idea, studying the idea, identifying its uniqueness and commercial prospects. The owner also needs to take care that the idea does not create unfair completion and provides a competitive product in the market, is free riding, meets or exceed customer needs, and fills the gap for a necessary product. In a second step it includes a method of selecting a tool for protecting the idea based on protection offered, period of validity, geographical limits, enforcement features, licensing issues and benefit sharing, takes cognizance of bilateral or regional or international treaties, and other legal implications. In a third step the owner of the idea needs to determine the type of intellectual property right that the idea falls under, i.e., patent, trademark, design, geographical indication, copyright, trade secret, integrated circuits, and plant breeder rights being statutorily the currently identified intellectual property rights. The owner of the idea may then proceed to secure the idea under the appropriate intellectual property right, to help the generator of the idea and his assignees to make a profitable business venture of the recognized idea.

Under intellectual property law, owners are granted certain exclusive rights to a variety of intangible assets such as musical, literary, and artistic works; discoveries and inventions; and words, phrases, symbols, and designs. If the idea is of a technical nature a patent is in order. If the idea is for branding a product or service a trademark is preferable. If the idea is on the aesthetic features of a product, in India, it is subject matter of a design patent. If the idea provides a particular product identified with particular characteristics belongto a geographical location then application can be made for securing a geographical indication certificate for the product. Thus the different types of intellectual property cover different subject matter and offer different types of rights to the owner. Accordingly there is a need for different methods of managing the intellectual property rights and thus enabling the intellectual property owner to exercise his rights and use his intellectual property in a profitable manner.

One has however to acknowledge that it may not be possible to develop Intellectual property management methods in silos. The methods need to take in to account culture, ideologies and types of intellectual property, valuation methods of intellectual property including disparities and economic significance, external corporate and organizational strategies; licensing in and out, strategic alliances, cooperative research and development, technology transfer, and intellectual property litigation, internal corporate and organizational strategies: stimulating inventions, competitive analysis and intellectual property exploitation, and decision-making on intellectual property commercialization, global piracy and corporate and organizational strategies, the impacts of intellectual property on mergers and acquisitions, the impacts of intellectual property on firm internationalization, and intellectual property and its effects on international negotiations among others.

Further, as mentioned above for securing an idea its commercial viability is a key parameter, for only a useful idea is worth securing. Securing the idea is a key link as premature disclosure of the idea will greatly erode its monetary value. However, since securing is a much latter step in the process of intellectual property management keeping the idea from being disclosed is a key link in the process. Further if the idea belongs to an industry where every idea is obsolete within a very short time of its generation then the entire process till securing has to be put on a fast track to enable the innovator and his assignees to enjoy the fruit of their hard work. Thus factors responsible for ensuring that the securing process is accelerated include change in public demand, short product cycle, productivity, appropriately skilled human resources, competition in the global and national markets and at times change in organizational and governmental policies. Accordingly the idea owner may be guided to make the right choice for his idea and deciding when and how the idea needs to be secured as an intellectual property right.

Managing an Intellectual Property Strategy

An intellectualproperty strategy aligned to a business strategy would be an ideal manner to drive a business. However in the real world typically IP issues drive most strategic considerations in an organisation. For example, many pharmaceutical & chemical companies that manufacture generic products the focus of their research revolve around reverse engineering compounds developed by innovator companies, that will lose their intellectual property protection and hence for which the generic companies would have freedom to operate. Their IP strategy is thus based on lapsing, abandoning, or expiring of patents belonging to innovator companies.

To a great extent an IP strategy will depend on the type of Organisation that is developing and employing the IP strategy. The environment in which the organisation operates also has an important say in developing the IP strategy.

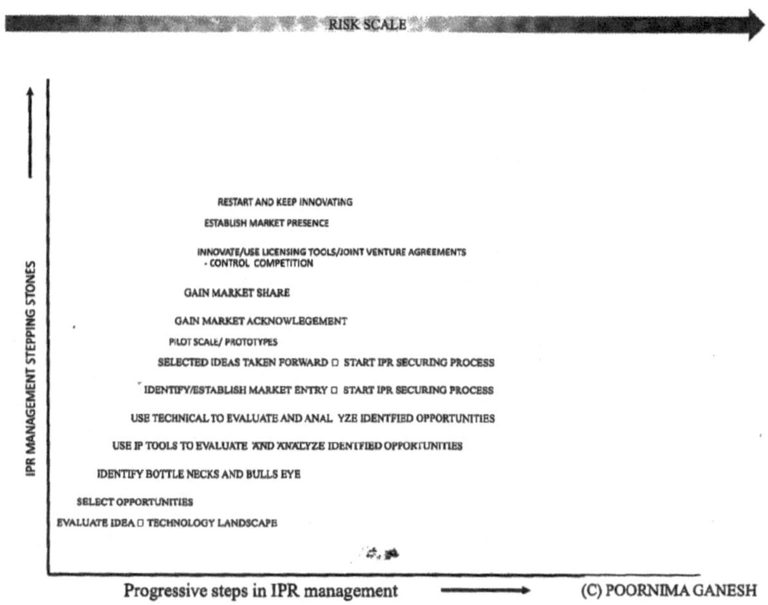

Fig. 1: IPR Enabled Knowledge Incubation and Wealth Realisation

Types of Organization and appropriate IP strategy

- Individual idea generators often look forward to partnering with commercial partners having a good reputation in the market to enable their ideas to become a reality. This is so because they often lack independent resources such as money, expertise, staff or distribution outlets. To make a profitable business venture of their ideas they may only need to know the methods of attract a commercial partner to provide the resources, for example by using licensing methods. A comprehensive intellectual property strategy or policy may not necessarily be what they are looking for.
- For Small to Medium Enterprises, internal structures need to allow for growth. There are fewer decision makers at the top which makes it much faster to come up with their comprehensive intellectual property strategy or policy. They also have sufficient resources and hence great opportunities to instil an effective intellectual property framework and tend to be quick adopters of intellectual property policies.
- Research organisations invariably have issues surrounding their researchers' desire to publish their ideas and gain a name in the world of science rather than making a business of their ideas. However this issue is fast becoming obsolete as more research organizations and universities are becoming more intellectual propertysavvy and are seeking to partner or collaborate with corporations and business ventures to make their ideas a reality. The pitfall

of these partnerships or collaborations is that they are built on research contracts where ownership of the resulting intellectual property can be ambiguous. Therefore an intellectual property strategy must include a stringent publication policy, an ownership policy and associated template agreements, a training policy to increase the awareness of intellectual property amongst the research staff as well as means to encourage them to communicate intellectual property issues to their commercial arm.

- Corporations are often large and unwieldy. The sheer size and diversity of organizations becomes a driver for establishing a comprehensive intellectual property strategy or policy. The intellectual property strategy needs to have firm guidelines about management responsibilities, employee responsibilities and communication throughout the organisation to ensure that there is a consistent overall approach to IP issues. This is where either in-house counsel or a strong relationship with an intellectual property firm can be invaluable. Regular intellectual property strategy meetings including members from different departments like research and development, technical, legal, and finance can help considerably here.

The following discussion will highlight the **steps involved in managing an intellectual property** in the form of a Patent or a Trademark.

A patent is one of the most widely prevailing and accepted method of protecting technical ideas and inventions. The term “patent” is derived from the latin word “patere” that means to lay open. Patentas we know is an exclusive right granted by a country to the owner of an invention in exchange for “laying open” is invention to the public. The exclusive rights is directed to allow the owner to make,use, manufacture, and market, or license, gift, assign, sell, or will the patented invention, provided the invention satisfies certain conditionsstipulated in the law. Exclusive right implies that no one else can make, use, manufacture ormarket the invention without the consent of the patent holder. This right is available for alimited period of time. In spite of the ownership of the rights, the use or exploitation of the rightsby the owner of the patent may not be possible due to other laws of the country which hasawarded the patent. These laws may relate to health, safety, food, security etc. As the right is conferred by the country,it can be revoked by the country under very special circumstances even if the patent has been soldor licensed or manufactured or marketed in the meantime. The patent right is territorial in natureand inventors/their assignees will have to file separate patent applications in countries of their interest, along with necessary fees, for obtaining patents in those countries.

Managing your intellectual property in the form of patents may be dependent on many factors, some of them being the type of invention, the domain of the invention, the market demand, competition, and also to some extent financial status of the owner. Managing of Patents may be discussed under different heads that are directly related with the different stages involved in the process of obtaining a grant for a patent.

Managing Idea Generation

Ideas may be generated either serendipitously or in a planned manner. Serendipitous ideas clearly mean ideas that just come up in an individual's mind or he is working towards an idea and observes an occurrence which he identifies as a new idea. These ideas are unexpected and may or may not happen.

Planned ideas may be obtained by creating a landscape for a portfolio of interest, for example, consider an organization working for cancer related drugs of a particular chemistry or drugs for a particular part of the body. A landscape may be prepared by searching the appropriate databases for patent and non-patent literature. The landscape may be broad, say any cancer drug, any chemistry or any body part or the landscape may be narrow, say a cancer drug having a particular chemistry affecting a particular body part.The landscape provides a clear picture of current state in the industry and technical area of choice, information on the strength and weakness of competitors, advancements made in a particular area, and areas where there is not much activity among others. Using the information from the landscape and having a knowledge of once own capabilities and industry, one can come up with useful and/or patentable ideas.

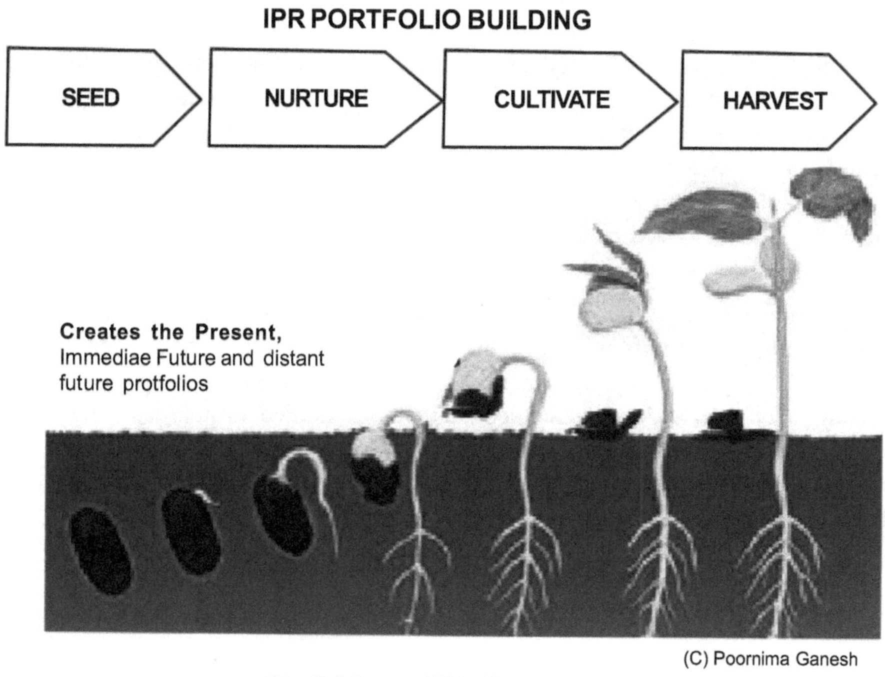

Fig. 2: Measure IP Perforance

Managing filtration of workable ideas

It is expensive and difficult to grow a business that has a weak intellectual property position as a consequence of developing unprotectable products. Filtration of ideas made on the basis of the idea being a patentable subject matter, an idea that can be actuated, or an idea that may be commercially viable may make an idea more successful. Ideally an idea that goes through these three evaluation techniques may be seed a prospective business venture.

Patentable Subject Matter

Not all ideas thought out by individuals or individuals in organizations may be worthy of being patentable subject matter. As per the patent law in almost all countries, any subject matter which is available in a published form, before the date of filing of a patent application, and any subject matter available in an unpublished patent application before the date of filing of a patent application may render the subject matter non-patentable. Moreover all nations have a list of non-patentable subject matter, like Section 3 and 4 in the Indian patent act. Accordingly, the ideas identified in the disclosures need to be evaluated for their patentability before being converted into the subject matter of a patent application.

Commercial prospects

If the idea is from a core portfolio then the commercial viability and market endearability of the idea will be another decisive factor in filtering the idea. Questions that may require answers include, how much new investment is required to make the idea commercial? or minor modifications in the existing set up will suffice?. If the idea is from a non-core or unrelated portfolio it need not be discarded, for if the idea has a commercial viability, licensing methods can be used to make the idea a profitable venture.

Actuable Idea

Research and development techniques may be employed to determine if the idea can be actuated. Reproduction of the idea will vindicate that the idea can be actuated. If the idea was discovered serendipitously then again reproduction of the idea will vindicate the idea. Once the idea is validated, prototypes of the ideas can be made in pilot production steps. The prototypes may be used for sensing market and market acceptability. Market acceptability paves way for large scale business opportunity and success in the business.

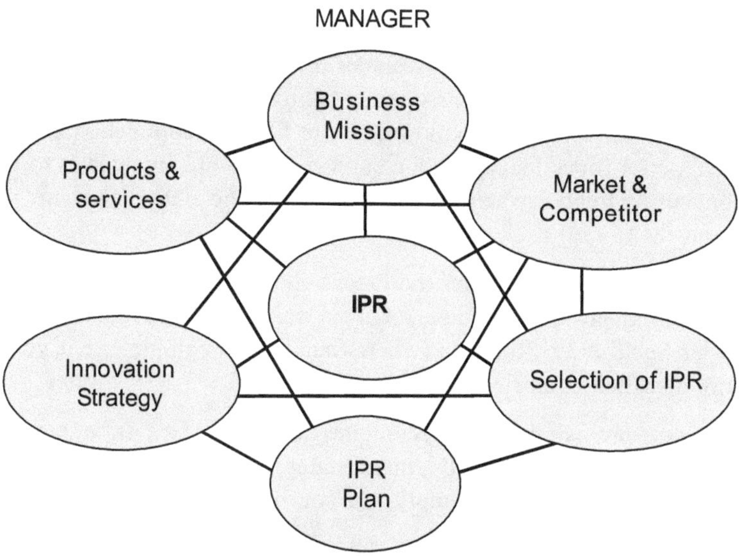

Fig. 3: Frame work

Managing Disclosure of Idea

Maintaining the security of your idea, till the idea is captured in a filed patent application is of primary importance. The environment in which you disclose your idea may either maintain the sanctity of your idea or may lead to the anticipation of your idea by public disclosure. Following the steps discussed below may give them better security for the idea that include both statutory and non-statutory methods of protecting your idea, but are necessarily exhaustive.

If the owner of the idea is an independent individual or a group of individuals or their respective assignees:

- Non-statutory Methods
- Capture the idea in the form of a disclosure with the date of the invention.
- To have a non disclosure agreement in place, before discussing the idea with anyone else, say for example, disclosing in a conference or workshop, in a journal article, another person, firm, patent agent or attorney, prospective client, prospective manufacturer, prospective licensee, etc., anybody other than the persons involved with the idea.

Statutory Methods

- Filing an application with any one of the convention countries, keeping in mind the national laws, for example, taking a waiver with the Indian Patent Office under Section 39, Rule 71, before filing an application in any one of the patent offices located in the countries who are signatories to the Paris convention treaty; (when your idea is a complete and you are sure in which countries to file)
- Filing an application under the Patent cooperation treaty keeping in mind the national laws, for example, taking a waiver with the Indian Patent Office under Section 39, Rule 71; (when your idea is complete, but you are not sure in which countries to file)
- Using the provisional filing techniques allowed by law, more specifically by the Patent law of India and United States; (when your idea is in the initial stages, but the scope is complete in your intellect)

If the owner of the idea is an organization or their respective assignees

- Non-statutory Methods
- Capture the idea in the form of a disclosure with the date of the invention and the names of all the idea providers.
- To have a non-disclosure agreement in place, before discussing the idea with anyone else, say for example, disclosing in a conference or workshop, in a journal article, another person, firm, patent agent or attorney, prospective client, prospective manufacturer, prospective licensee, etc., as far as possible restricting the dissemination of any information on the idea to the group of people who came up with the idea in the first place, anybody outside the organization.
- Have an organization-employee agreement to ensure restricted dissemination of information.

Statutory Methods

- Filing an application with any one of the convention countries, keeping in mind the national laws, for example, taking a waiver with the Indian Patent Office under Section 39, Rule 71, before filing an application in any one of the patent offices located in the countries who are signatories to the Paris convention treaty; (when your idea is a complete and you are sure in which countries to file)
- Filing an application under the patent cooperation treaty keeping in mind the national laws, for example, taking a waiver with the Indian Patent Office

under Section 39, Rule 71; (when your idea is complete, but you are not sure in which countries to file)

- Using the provisional filing techniques allowed by law, more specifically by the Patent law of India and United States; (when your idea is in the initial stages, but the scope is complete in your intellect)

The non-statutory method of protecting the idea is preferably a must do step irrespective of whether the idea is convertible to a business proposition or successful business. However, the statutory method of protecting the idea may be extended only to those ideas that are proven to be convertible to a business proposition or successful business.

Managing appropriate filing time

Time consideration is an important aspect when protecting an idea statutorily or non-statutorily. The time is also dependent on the technical domain to which the idea belongs and the organization responsible for generating the idea. For example, pharmaceutical and life science research organizations usually have greater developmental time than software companies. As discussed in the statutory filing applications above it is possible to delay filing applications or shift filing dates of applications if a particular project is taking time to become market ready. Further, the intellectual property policy of the organization should include a mandate that marketing and research cannot publish until the IP position has been clearly considered.

Managing Motivation of inventors

Every individual and individuals in organizations may come with a variety of ideas while involved in their routine working schedules. These ideas may include new products, new processes, new methods, new systems, new uses, new analytical methods, etc.. The individuals should be encouraged to come up with more ideas by providing some kind of incentives and motivation will definitely.

Managing Infringement of Patents

Infringement management can be classified into two aspects i.e., Avoiding infringement and disallowing infringement

Managing the Freedom to Market or practice – Avoiding infringement.

It can be financially disastrous to invest heavily in a marketing campaign or product manufacture to find that you cannot enter a market because of freedom to market issues. Then, there is the loss of reputation if you have to recall a product. Plus it is disappointing to miss out on an opportunity because the wider application of an idea is not identified.

As we have discussed above a Patent application is typically filed at the beginning of a product or a process development process when the scope of the idea is clear. The Patent application thus typically contains claims and experimental or drawing sections based on the initial working of the idea. During the prosecution of the patent application at the patent offices where the patent application has been filed, the claims may see a sea change based on the prior art references quoted by the examiner. The patentability check that the owner of the patent application carries out before filing may or may not include the same prior art references quoted by the examiner. Accordingly the claims may need modification in the prosecution process and the final claims may be relatively narrower than the filed claims. Furthermore when the product or process goes through the process development step from small scale to large scale i.e., in the pilot studies and then during the large scale manufacture, some fine tuning may be in order to actuate the idea. The fine tuning may lead to a product or process that is not exactly the same as the one claimed, but still within the scope. Before launching any product in the market, it will be an ideal step to undertake a freedom to practice search and ensure that your product is not infringing any granted patent that is still enjoying the grant status in the country where the product is to be potentially marketed. The freedom to practice search goes a long way in limiting the liability of any potential infringement, as this search is considered as a due diligence search. The search is typically signed off by an advocate or attorney in law who certify that to the best of his client's knowledge the marketed product is not disclosed in a granted patent as mentioned above.

The freedom to market or practice opinion is more important in situations where the person undertaking to manufacture or market the product does not have a granted patent for the idea in question.

Managing infringement by others – disallowing infringement

This leads to a question "To Patent or to maintain as trade secret?" Though there is greater awareness and understanding in the field of patents, there are many inventors who are still not comfortable about disclosing their ideas to the public even in the form of patent applications/patent. This aversion to filing patent applications may stem from the fact that in many developing nations enforceability of patents is still a challenge. To start with it is not only difficult but also at times impossible to detect infringement of patents. Many a time after detection the inventor or applicant may not have sufficient financial resources to fight for his rights.

A lot depends on what your patent claims cover i.e., product, process, method, system, or use claims. For example your claims are directed to a product and if an infringer markets the same product it is not very difficult to detect infringement. In this situation, the financial resource of the innovator will be a foremost reason to pursue or not pursue enforcement. On the other hand, if the claims are directed to a process and the product from this process are not having an identifiable signature, it will be practically impossible to detect infringement. If detecting infringement is impossible, it would be advisable for the idea owner to maintain the idea as a trade secret. The most famous trade secrets known in the industry include those of Coco Cola, and KFC (Kentucky Fried chicken) recipes. Furthermore, certain subject matters are not patentable and hence become subject matter of Trade Secrets.

Enforceability of the patent owner's rights may be achieved using different methods. A patent owner may choose to enforce owner's rights by giving a notice to the alleged infringer and taking the matter to a court. The alleged infringer on the other hand may choose to make an attempt to invalidate the patent in court. Parties with strong financial back up may go for this method. This choice made by the patent owner and the alleged infringer may lead to a long and torturous legal battle for both parties. Quicker resolution methods may be followed by either or both parties. The alleged infringer may agree to stop infringing. The patent owner and the alleged infringer may decide to settle out of court. The patent owner may agree to provide a licence to the alleged infringer. The quicker resolution methods are generally beneficial to both parties.

OPTIONS AVAILABLE TO OWNER

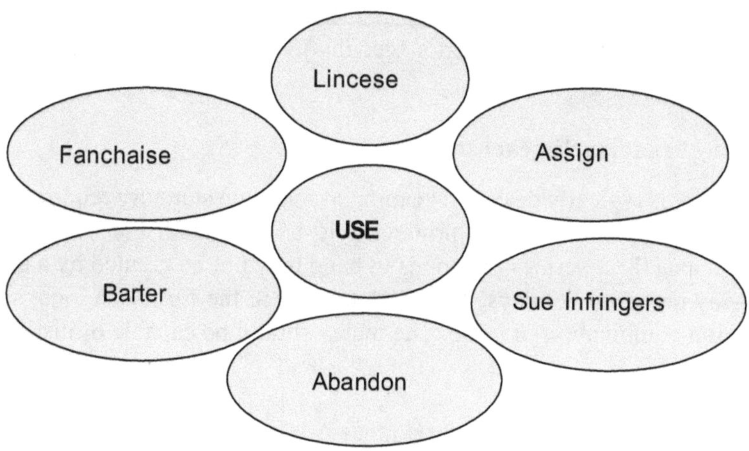

Fig. 4: Options available to owner

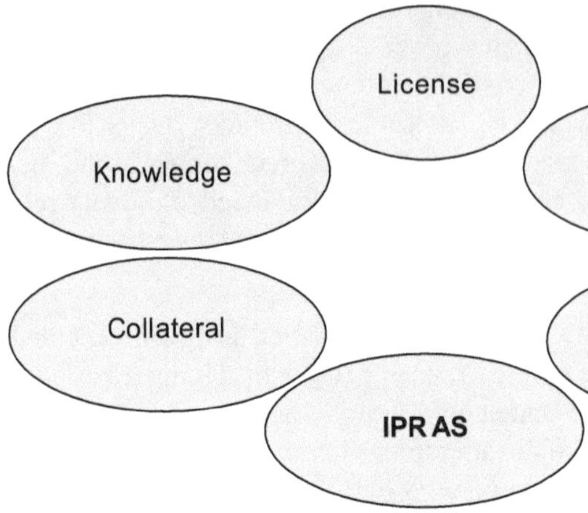

Fig. 5: Realising value of IPR

Contrary to a patent a trademark is an accepted method for protecting a brand. A trademark, trade mark, or trade-mark is a distinctive sign or indicator used by an individual, business organization, or other legal entity to identify that the products or services to consumers with which the trademark appears originate from a unique source, and to distinguish its products or services from those of other entities. Managing your intellectual property in the form of a trade mark may also be dependent on many factors, some of them being the type of product, region where the good is to be marketed, and also to some extent financial status of the owner. Managing of trademarks may be discussed under different heads that are directly related with the different stages involved in the process of obtaining a grant for a trademark.

Managing trademark generation

A trademark is typically designed keeping in mind the statutory requirements, the product, and region where the product is to be marketed. For example a trade mark that exactly describes the goods in hand may not be granted by a trademark office, say the word holidays. The mark may be in the form of a logo, a word, a phrase or a combination of these. The marks should be capable of distinguishing the goods.

Managing filtration of trademark ideas

Most of the trademark offices in the world offer public search windows. Before applying for registration of a mark, it would be wise for the owner to determine that his trade mark or a similar mark is not registered in the database of the country where the proposed mark is to be applied for. Trademarks fall under a variety of classes depending on the product. For example food and textiles will not fall under the same class. So the determination discussed above will have to be made for the mark in the classification that describes the product in question.

Managing infringement of trademarks

Unlike a patent a trademark need not be filed before disclosing the mark to secure statutory protection. Good will generated by continuous use of the trade mark is also qualified to be granted legal protection in case of misuse or wrongful use of the mark. It is however advisable to register the mark, since settling an infringement case based on good will may prove to be tortuous as the owner has to prove beyond doubt that the mark in question has been used by the owner prior to that of the alleged infringer.

Use of same or similar marks may be construed as "passing off" of his goods as the owners goods by the alleged infringer. Similar issues may exist in identifying such infringements as in case of patents. The owner of the mark needs to have a mechanism where the products in his class are monitored on a regular basis and any identical or similar mark user is challenged. This again depends on the financial resources of the trademark owner. Enforceability of the trademark owner's rights may be achieved using different methods. A trademark owner may choose to enforce owner's rights by giving a notice to the alleged infringer and taking the matter to a court. The alleged infringer on the other hand may choose to make an attempt to prove that the mark was in use much before the first date of use by the owner either by others or by the alleged infringer. Parties with strong financial back up may go for this method. This choice made by the trademark owner and the alleged infringer may lead to a long and torturous legal battle for both parties. Quicker resolution methods may be followed by either or both parties. The alleged infringer may agree to stop infringing. The trademark owner and the alleged infringer may decide to settle out of court. The trademark owner may agree to provide a licence to the alleged infringer. The quicker resolution methods are generally beneficial to both parties.

The other intellectual properties mentioned herein may also be managed keeping in mind the statutory and non-statutory requirements to manage the intellectual property of choice.

Managing the profitable exploitation of intellectual property

The options available to the owner of an intellectual property are varied. The owner can use, license, franchise, barter, assign, sue infringers, gift, will or abandon the property. The intellectual property can also be valued as asset in the form of knowledge, insurance, collateral, and property. These options are available for all the different forms of intellectual properties mentioned in this article.

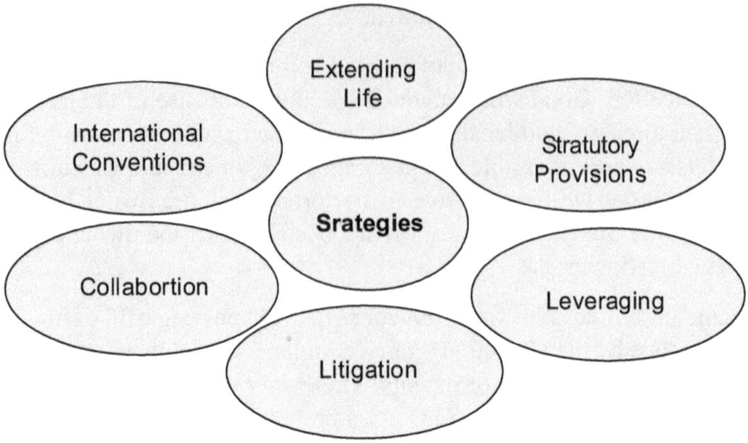

Fig. 6: Strategic IP

Managing an Exit Strategy

It is but a natural course that products enter the market based on demand and may need to exit the market when the demand fades out, i.e. product lifespan may be very short. The exit of products from the market may also depend on the organizational policies, national policies, and international policies. For example, some pharmaceutical products get launched with great aplomb in the market for a particular indication. Later on after some years of usage, negative effects of the drug may be observed which was not earlier detected during the clinical studies. Such kinds of drugs are compulsorily pulled out of the market. For short lived products, either formal intellectual property protection is forsaken, or quick fix deterrent applications may be useful in order to buy enough time to exploit a market. Companies in for the long haul require a well-managed process that is mindful of budget constraints and tailored to the companies aspirations for expansion. A large impressive intellectual property portfolio helps if a trade sale is planned. Patent and trade mark applications can be timed so that you are not committed to completing the applications before the actual sale – thus avoiding major costs.

Conclusion

New thoughts and new possibilities will continue to being explored as long as human life exists. There will thus always be a need for management of the subsequently generated intellectual property rights. Ideal management of intellectual property will enable us to enhance the critical understanding of intellectual property in theory and practice, to appreciate the strategic importance of intellectual property to corporate and organisational success, and to disseminate knowledge on the management of intellectual property and commercialisation of different forms of intellectual property. The steps and methods discussed above are based on experiences in the intellectual property industry today.

10

Patent Infringement — An Overview

Rajeshwari Hariharan

Abstract

Patent infringement is the act of unauthorized making, using, offering for sale or selling any patented invention within the India. In case of patent infringement it is necessary for the patentee to compare the claims granted to him with the allegedly infringing product an check whether there is an infringement – whether the infringing product falls within the scope of the claims of the patent. In such a case the patentee may sue for relief in an appropriate court. The patentee may ask for permanent injunction and damages on account of the infringement. It is the crusade of the inventor asserting his rights against an infringer and the law recognizes the importance of this right; because, without such positive and assertive rights, industrial progress would be hard to come by

What is a Patent?

The basic goal behind grant of patents is to promote technical advancement and industrial development by introducing new technological innovations and to encourage scientific spirit. That is why a patentee is granted limited monopoly in exchange of full public disclosure of his invention. During the period in which the patent is valid, the patentee has the right to stop any third party from breaching the monopoly granted to him. Thereafter, when the patent expires, the patented invention passes into public domain and everyone is free to practice the invention which originally belonged to the patentee.

Scope of Patent rights under Indian law

It is important to understand the scope of rights granted when someone is granted a patent. The Patents Act does not provide for a bundle of positive rights in favour of the patentee. Rather, it provides vide Section 48 that patents granted in India confer upon the patent holder an exclusive exclusionary right, a negative right, under which, no third party can exercise the make, use, offer for sale, sell or import the subject matter of the patent. This exclusion extends to both product patents and patents which claim a process. Therefore grant of patent is not an attempt to legitimize the making of the invention by the patentee but a right to the patentee to stop others/third parties from using his invention without his consent.

It is important to understand that absence of patent does not mean the patentee cannot practice his invention, he can do so; however he cannot prevent other parties from using his invention.

Patent claims

Patent claims play a very important role in patent law. As stated earlier, the monopoly granted in respect of a patent is defined by the claims that are granted. By virtue of a claim, the patentee tells the world what the patentee wishes the patent to protect and what third parties should not practice. Hence, a product would be infringing only if it falls within the scope of the claim granted.

For instance, if a claim states

"A herbal composition comprising extract of turmeric, tamarind, gingiber and piper nigrum for treatment of osteoporosis".

And if a third party was to prepare a composition which contains extracts of turmeric, terminalia chebulia,, tulsi, and piper nigrum.

Then the composition of the third party would be considered different by the court and no action would lie. Similarly if the patentee had described two compositions, and claimed only one, then third parties can practice the composition not claimed and the patentee cannot maintain any action. Therefore, the entire basis of infringement is founded on the claims and it is also why claims are very important.

Remedies in case of infringement

In case an instance of infringement is found, then one may either send a notice to the third party advising him that his activities amount to infringement and call upon the party not to continue these acts any further. In most instances, the infringer may not respond to the notice and cease the infringing activities. Hence the patentee would have to file a suit for patent infringement against the infringer. Such a suit for infringement may be filed in a district court having jurisdiction to try the suit.

The suit can be file in that court where the cause of action has arisen or where the defendant/infringer resides or carries on business. It can be filed at a place where the infringing goods are found.

As an example, if a patent has been granted and if the defendant company has its office at Calcutta, however the infringing products are available not only in Calcutta but also Delhi, then the suit for infringement may be filed at Calcutta or at Delhi.

Once such a suit is filed the Court will cal upon the infringer to explain by filing reply his stand and position. In patent infringement cases it is not uncommon for the defendant to challenge the validity of the patent itself. The alleged infringer may take various defences including that the patent itself is invalid and should not to have been granted and there is no question of infringement. In such cases where the defendant takes invalidity of the patent as a defense to infringement and counter claims for revocation/cancellation of the patent is filed, the case instead of being tried in the District Court is transferred from the District Court to the appropriate High Court.

When suit for infringement can be filed

It is only after a patent has been granted that a party can institute a suit for infringement. Applicants for patent cannot institute a suit during the interim period when the patent is being prosecuted before the Patent Office i.e. the period from when the patent specification is filed till the actual grant of the patent. But, damages sustained due to the infringement, committed during the period i.e., between the date of publication of complete specification and the date of grant, may be claimed after a suit for infringement has been instituted.

Comparison of infringing device and claims

Infringement is first seen by comparison of the allegedly infringing product/process with independent or stand alone claims. To make out a case for infringement the device or product which is alleged to be infringing should fall within the four corners of at least one independent claim that has been granted. An allegedly infringing product or process should be compared with the granted claims in the patent-in-suit and not with a preferred embodiment i.e. one of the preferred examples provided in the specification or with a commercialized embodiment of the patent. This is important because what the patentee brings to the market might be distinct from the invention as claimed in the patent. The scope of monopoly or the right to exclude is not determined not by product in the market but by the claims of the patent.

Types of infringement

a) Direct and Literal infringement

Literal infringement is found where every limitation of the claim is found in the allegedly infringing device literally i.e the allegedly infringing product falls wholly within the scope a granted claim and has all elements of the claim. Infringement is avoided if even one feature recited in a claim does not appear in the product. If every element of a claim is used in a product, infringement is said to be "literal".

As an example, if the claim is for a " A herbal composition comprising extract of turmeric, tamarind, gingiber and piper nigrum for treatment of osteoporosis" and the alleged infringer also produces a herbal composition containing all these elements, then it is a case of direct or literal infringement.

b) Equivalent

The doctrine of equivalents is a rule, developed by the courts in USA, that allows a court to hold a party liable for patent infringement even though the infringing device or process does not fall within the literal scope of a patent claim, but nevertheless is equivalent to the claimed invention. The legal test, articulated in the case of Graver Tank & Manufacturing Co. v. Linde Air Products Co., (Citation: 339 U.S. 605 (1950)), is whether the difference between the limitation in the accused device and the limitation literally recited in the patent claim is "insubstantial". The test applied to judge whether the "difference" is insubstantial is called the triple-identity test. Under this test, the difference between the limitation in the accused device and the limitation literally recited in the patent claim may be found to be "insubstantial" if the limitation in the accused device:

1. Performs substantially the same function
2. In substantially the same way
3. To yield substantially the same result
4. As the limitation literally recited in the patent claim.

For example, consider a simple hypothetical patent claiming a metal door knob designed to be used in opening and closing the door. Now, if another party subsequently began producing a door knob that was exactly like the claimed metal door knob in every respect, except that it was made of some different material (that nevertheless performed substantially the same function in the same way to achieve the same result as metal i.e opened the door efficiently), it is apt to say that the original patent's claim scope should be enlarged by the doctrine of equivalents to cover the copy, which differed only with regard to the substance used in its manufacture.

Procedure followed by the court in case of infringement

Whenever the court receives a case of infringement of patent, the court will call upon the allegedly infringing party to file its written reply alongwith any documentary evidence. Thereafter, after the parties have completed the pleadings, the court will frame the issues that have arisen in the case. The matter will proceed for trial wherein oral evidence of both parties will be taken. At the end of this process, oral arguments would be made by both parties and the court will then pronounce its verdict. If the court is convinced about the infringement, Court has the discretion to award damages and costs to the party who holds a patent.

Exceptions to infringement

Every activity is not an act of infringement and there are some exceptions provided in law; these include:

1. Any act of making, constructing, using a patented invention for purposes of research, teaching or allied reasons would not amount to infringement. Hence, if a chemical compound is patented, it is not an act of infringement if that product was produced by a research laboratory for further investigations and for making further improvements or even for teaching.
2. Use of a patented invention solely for purposes of obtaining regulatory permissions whether in India or elsewhere would also not be deemed to be an act of infringement.

Infringement Cases in India

In India, there have not been too many cases of patent infringement; partly because, prior to 2005, India followed the process patent regime and the term of patent itself was only 7 years- the time taken to grant a patent in India was quite long and enforcement was meaningless. However, now with the product patent regime in place, the situation is now changing and many companies are obtaining patents and trying to enforce their rights.

Some examples of patent infringement cases

a) Strix Ltd v Maharaja Appliances Ltd (6.11.2009) (Delhi High Court order)

Strix Ltd is a maker of electric kettles and other electrical applicances. Strix filed a suit in the Delhi High Court alleging that Maharaja Applicances had infringed their intellectual property rights, in Indian patent no.192511 by manufacturing and marketing a similar product. Maharaja took the defence that the patent is invalid and should not have been granted in the first place. However the Delhi High court was not persuaded. The Delhi High Court the Court observed that Maharaja had failed to discharge its burden of raising a 'creditable challenge' to the validity of the Strix patent and failed to support such challenge with scientific material, supported or explained by the evidence of an expert. Further, the court observed the burden on the defendant to show that it has put forward a creditable challenge to the patent will be greater because there was no opposition filed to challenge Strix's patent. Eventually the court granted interim injunction restraining Maharaja Appliances from manufacturing and marketing Maharaja Whiteline electric kettle Model No EK 172 as it infringed Strix's patent IN 192511.

b) Raj Praksh Vs Mangat Ram

This case involved a patent relating to a process for printing picture films for use in film-strip viewer and the films made by the process. The patent holder, sued the infringer, who were making and selling similar film strip viewers for patent infringement. The Court compared the product of the defendants with the patent claims and held them liable for infringement because Defendants were also selling viewers with similar films as that of the patent holder. Though the Defendants made certain variations in their film viewers, the Court stated that such changes were unessential to the invention and the viewers of the patent holder and the defendants were substantially the same. This was one case wherein the court upheld the principle of equivalence and upheld patent infringement.

Conclusion

Obtaining a patent is very important; equally important is the aspect of safeguarding the patent and making sure that infringers do not trespass into the patented area and make undue profit. Hence an inventor must be vigilant and take steps to curtail and curb infringement.

11

Patent Search and Examination Methodologies

S.K. Swarup

Abstract

Patent is a monopoly right which is granted by the Government to the applicant for the full disclosure of an 'invention' which is 'new', 'inventive' and 'industrially applicable'. Thus, before filing a patent application, the inventor must be sure that the work done by him is new and inventive. Further, during the examination of the patent application, it is required to be verified that the invention claimed in the disclosure/specification is new, inventive and industrially applicable. Since the search for the 'Novelty' of the invention is carried worldwide, it becomes all the more important for the inventor and the examiners to search for the prior art thoroughly. Searching for the prior art (i.e. state of the art) across the globe in around millions of documents both patents and non-patent documents, is like 'searching a needle in the haystack'*. However, by using proper keywords and classification techniques, it is possible to arrive at the closest prior art available. Each patent application is classified by the Indian Patent Office and thus attributed to one or several fields of technology. The classification scheme applied is the International Patent Classification (IPC).*

The International Patent Classification (IPC) is a system of keeping patent information related to different fields of technology at appropriate place. It is analogous to a library where the books are kept in an order where they can be easily searched as per the requirements. The IPC is all the more important since millions of documents are added every day and without such system like IPC in place, it is very difficult to ascertain the 'state of art' which is of prime importance to determine the 'Novelty' of the invention. The IPC is a hierarchical classification system which uses symbols to map all fields of technologies. Since the IPC uses symbols to map the technologies, it is a language independent system and hence serves as an important search tool for the users of patent information worldwide.

Conducting Patent Search

Patent is granted to inventions which are 'New', 'Inventive' and 'Industrially applicable'. Thus to ascertain that the invention is 'New' and 'Inventive' it is important to search the closest prior art and then analyze the invention with respect to the closest prior art. The search for the closest prior art has different meaning for different people. For example, the patent examiner determines the novelty of the invention in order to grant or refuse a patent. For some, it is a tool which can determine whether a patent can be opposed or invalidated. Further, it can be used to ascertain whether you have freedom to operate on certain patents. Thus different people have different objectives of using patent search.

Patent Databases

- **Some examples of Free database**
  - Espacenet
  - Free patents online
  - United States Public Pair database
  - Google patents
  - Patent Lens
- **Some examples of paid databases**
  - Thompson Innovation
  - STN
  - Delphion
  - Quetsel / Orbit
  - Derwent World Patent Index (DWPI)

Patent search strategies

To begin with the search for the prior art, the user must first decide upon a search strategy. The user must be clear about the terminologies used in relation to the invention and therefore must use as many synonyms, variation in spellings etc., as possible in the search strings. Various types of strategies that are commonly used are given below:

a. Key string search
b. Patent classification search
c. Citation based search
d. Assignee and/or Inventor based search

By intelligent use of the aforementioned search strategies in different combinations, several queries can be constructed to arrive at the closest prior art.

a. Key string search

A key string search is a method of searching database key words. The process of carrying a keyword search is given below:

- Identify key words that define the features of invention
- Identify different synonyms or acronyms to the key words
- Form key strings that can be used as a search query in the database:
- Combine synonymous words using OR operator. For example, a search query such as (latch OR lock) will return results, which have the word "latch" or "lock" or "latch" and "lock"
- Join combinations of words using AND operator. For example, a search query such as (latch OR lock) AND (rod OR bar) will return documents which have one or more of "latch" and "lock" AND one or more of "rod" and "bar"
- If time is a constraint, then you can start with a narrow search query and then decide on broadening the query depending on the results you find.
- Key word search can be very tedious. Successful key word searching depends on the exhaustiveness of the key words used. For example, if you are searching for documents relating to *pen* by using only "*pen*" as your query, then you will miss documents, which in fact relates to *pen*, but they might have used the phrase *"writing instrument"* instead of *Pen*.

Thus, it can be inferred that using keywords alone, however carefully you construct the keywords, there is always a risk of missing some relevant results. Therefore, in order to get more relevant hits, we generally use the Patent Classification codes along with the keywords to arrive at better results.

b. Patent classification search

Patent Classification system uses the symbols to map all fields of technologies. Thus search for inventions in a particular field of technology can be done irrespective of language using the symbols. While classifying the invention, each invention is assigned a particular symbol representing the Section, Class, Subclass,

Main Groups, subgroups etc. Therefore, while searching for a particular invention, we look for a particular symbol i.e. Section /Class/ Subclass which is relevant for the invention to conduct a classification search.

Search using the International Patent Classification, can narrow down the result set as compared to what we get using the keyword search. However, a good combination of Keywords and IPC codes along with the use of different Boolean operators is more likely to fetch a record set having reasonable records. The user can then go through these records to ascertain whether the invention is the closest prior art or not.

There are several ways of identifying the relevant IPC codes for a particular invention, some of which are:

- The IPC system has eight sections and about 70000 subdivisions including various classes, subclasses, groups etc. Thus to identify the correct IPC, the user is required to browse the IPC within the relevant sections. However, this approach is sometimes tedious, especially for a person new to IPC.
- To overcome this problem, there is also provided a catchword index. The list of relevant catchwords can be accessed using the link *http://www.wipo.int/ipcpub/#&notion=cw*. The user can also type the catchword in the search box and is provided with the relevant IPC on that particular catchword. The user can subsequently browse through the classes listed under the selected catchwords to select relevant IPC codes.
- Using the relevant/related patent references that you found using key word search to identify relevant IPC codes.

The ideal way to perform a search is

- Use any of the aforementioned free patent databases with some relevant keywords.
- Browse the result-set obtained for some relevant hit.
- Browse through the relevant record to ascertain its IPC.
- Identify the relevant IPC codes and the go through the details of each IPC Code.
- Try to identify the relevant IPC code for your invention from the definitions of IPC codes
- Use the most relevant IPC code to search the invention.
- Additionally, use the relevant keyword in combination with relevant IPC code to get a manageable amount of relevant records.

c. Citation based search

Citations are references to the prior technologies. There can be a backward citation i.e. references which the patent document itself is citing and forward citations i.e. references that are citing the instant patent document. While performing the search, we can take help from these citations also. The IPC of the cited documents may also be used as a search parameter. The use of cited documents in search strategy helps bring out more relevant results which can be analyzed for determining novelty and inventive step.

d. Assignee/Applicant/inventor based search

The use of assignee/ inventor name in the search strategy can bring out the details of the inventions performed by the same inventor/assignee, which can provide further information as to which particular IPC the particular invention belongs.

Thus by intelligent use of the aforementioned search strategies, one can certainly find relevant prior art according to the need and objective of the searcher.

Benefits

- Helps identifying the closest prior art
- Helps inventors to identify the prior art before filing the application
- Help examiners evaluate patentability of an invention
- Helps reduce the grant of ineffective/frivolous patents.
- Helps appreciation of the technology using Patent Mapping/Plotting onto real-world objects.

12

International Patent Classification

Vimal Kumar Varun

Abstract

Describes the genesis, organization and Internet representation of International Patent Classification (IPC). Provides the outline of seventh edition and useful URLs related to it.

Keywords: International Patent Classification, Patent Classification, Classification, Internet representation

Introduction

The International Patent Classification, commonly known as the IPC, is based on an international multi-lateral treaty administered by World Intellectual Property Organization (WIPO). This treaty is called the Strasbourg Agreement concerning the IPC, which was concluded in 1971 and came into force on October 7, 1975. The Agreement aimed to overcome the difficulties caused by using diverse national patent classification system. The common classification system defined by the Agreement is applied to patent and utility model documents. The Agreement is open to States party to the Paris Convention for the Protection of Industrial Property.

Sixty two countries were members of the Strasbourg Union In July 2012. The list of members is regularly updated and details are available at *http://www.wipo.int/treaties/en/ShowResults.jsp?lang=en&treaty_id=11.*

The Organization of the IPC

The International Patent Classification (IPC), established by the Strasbourg Agreement 1971, provides for a hierarchical system of language independent symbols for the classification of patents and utility models according to the different areas of technology to which they pertain. The IPC is a hierarchical classification areas of technology to which they pertain. The IPC is a hierarchical classification system comprising **sections, classes, subclasses** and **groups** (main groups and subgroups). Every subdivision of the IPC is indiacated by a **symbol** and has a title.The appropriate IPC sysmbols are indicated on each patent document, of which more than 1,000,000 were issued each year in the last 10 years. The IPC symbols are allotted by the national or regional industrial property office that publishes the patent document. For PCT document, IPC symbols are allotted by the International Searching Authority (ISA)

The classification has been periodically revised in order to improve the system and to take account of technical development. It consists of **8** sections, **120** classes, 640 subclasses and about 70,000 groups. The IPC divides all technolgical fields into eight sections as shown in Table 1.

Table 1: Organization of the IPC

Sections	Subjects
A.	Human necessities
B.	Performing Operations; Transporting
C.	Chemistry; Metallurgy
D.	Textiles; Paper
E.	Fixed construction
F.	Mechanical engineering; Lighting; Heating; Weapons; Blasting
G.	Physics
H.	Electricity

Each section is subdivided into classes whose symbols consist of the section symbol followed by a two-digit number. In its turn, each class contain one or several subclasses whose symbols consist of the class symbol followed by a capital letter, for example, A 01 B.

Each subclass is broken down into subdivisions referred to as **groups**, which are either main groups or subgroups. Main group symbols consist of the subclass symbol followed by a one- to three-digit number, the oblique stroke and the number 00, for example, A 01 B 1/00.

Subgroups form subdivisions under the main groups. Each subgroup symbol includes the subclass symbol followed by the one- to three-digit number of its main group, the oblique stroke and a number of at least two digits other than 00, for example, A 01 B 1/02.

The title of a subgroup is preceded by one or more dots indicating the hierarchical position of that subgroup, i.e., indicating that each subgroup forms a subdivision of the nearest group above it having one dot less.

History of the IPC

The text of the first edition of the classification was established pursuant to the provisions of the European Convention on the International Classification of Patents for invention of 1954. Following the signing of the Strasbourg Agreement the International (European) Classification of Patents for Invention, which has been published on September 1, 1968 was as of March 24, 1971, considered and referred to as the first edition of the Classification. The first edition of the Calssification was in force from September 1, 1968 to June 30, 1974. The validity of different IPC editions is given in Table 2.

Table 2: Validity of the IPC Editions

No.	From	To
1.	September 1, 1968	June 30, 1974
2.	July 1, 1974	December 31, 1979
3.	January 1, 1980	December 31, 1984
4.	January 1, 1985	December 31, 1989
5.	January 1, 1990	December 31, 1994
6.	January 1, 1995	December 31, 1999
7.	January 1, 2000	December 31, 2005
8. (IPC 2006)	January 1, 2006	December 31, 2008
IPC 2009	Janauary1,2009	December 31, 2009
IPC 2010	January 1, 2010	December 31, 2010
IPC 2011	January 1, 2011	December 31, 2011
IPC 2012	January 1, 2012	December 31, 2012
IPC 2013	January 1, 2013	continues

The Classification was designed and developed for many years, mainly as a paper based information tool. Changes to the structure of the Classification and to methods of its revision and application were needed in order to ensure its efficient and effective use in the electronic environment. For this reason, member States of the IPC Union decided, in 1999, to launch a reform of the Classification and to introduce a transitional revision period during which, in parallel with revision of the Classification, the changes necessitated by the reform had to be elaborated. The transitional revision period started in 1999 and in 2005 the basic period of reform was completed. Following the reform of the IPC, for the editions that were in force from January 1,2006, to December 31,2010, the classification was divided into core and advanced levels. each edition of the core level was indicated by the year of entry into force of that edition. IPC-2006 was in force from January 1, 2006, to Devember 31, 2008, and IPC-2009 entered into force on January 1, 2009. Each new version of the advanced level of the IPC was indicated by the year and the month of the entry into force of that version, for example, IPC 2008.01. From January 1, 2011, onwards, the division of the Classification into core and advanced levels was discountinued and each new version of the IPC is indicated by the year and the month of the entry into force of that version, for example, IPC-2011.01.

The current edition of IPC 2013.01 (January1, 2013) is availabe at *http.// ww.wipo.int/classification/ipc/en/ITsupport/Version20130101/index.html and the earlier editions are available at http://www.wipo.int/classifiction/ipc/en/Tsupport/ versions.html.* Browse the current IPC and earlier editions at *http://web2.wipo.int/ ipcpub/.*

The Classification is indispensable for the retrieval of patent documents in the search for **Prior art.** Such retrieval is needed by patent-issuing authorities, potential inventors, research and development units, and others concerned with the application or development of technology.

The Guide to the IPC is available at *http://www.wipo.int/export/sites/www/ classifications/ipc/en/guide_ipc.pdf.*

Internet Presentation of the IPC

In the Internet presentation of the current version of the IPC, at http:// web2.wipo.int/ipcpub/#refresh=page, the index page includes a list of eight sections designated by letters A to H with the title of each section. After clicking on the relevant section, the contents of the section appear containing all classes and subclasses to which the section is subdivided. Having selected the relevant subclass, the user can navigate to its subdivisions and browse the groups included in the subclass until reaching the group covering the subject sought. The Internet version of the IPC also permits quick navigation in the text by using direct access ("Go to") to the relevant symbol of the Classification.

The hypertext links provided allow jumping from one language version (English or French) to the other by clicking on a flag located in front of main groups symbols. The similar manner of navigation is possible between IPC places interconnected by so-called references which represent phrases in brackets following a class, subclass or group title. Such a reference shows that the subject matter indicated by the reference is covered by the place (or places) referred to. A reference has the function of the limitation of scope or indication of precedence.

Having determined the essential characteristics of the technical subject which is being sought, it is necessary to locate in the IPC the appropriate place. To this end, a systematic approach should be adopted and followed step by step, i.e., the relevant section, class and subclass should first be identified and, then, the main group or the subgroup. It is particularly important to thoroughly read all the titles and explanatory notes, since they significantly affect the interpretation of the titles of subclasses, main groups and subgroups. The title of each subgroup must be read as being dependent upon, and restricted by, the titles of the higher level subgroups, the main group and the subclass. Bearing this in mind, it is necessary to select the lowest order (i.e., with the largest number of dots) subgroup which is still wide enough in scope to embrace all the essential characteristics of the subject in question.

For the uninitiated user, it is advisable to approach the Classification by using the official *Catchword Index to the IPC*. This publication contains thousands of catchwords representing specific technical terms used in patent documentation and technical literature, which are arranged in alphabetical order. Under the catchwords, the catchword phrases appear giving an indication of subject matter, which is designated by IPC symbols. It should be noted, however, that the Catchword Index in no sense replaces any part of the IPC and must not be read as modifying the effect of anything in the latter.

IPC Green Inventory

WIPO launched on September 16, 2010, an on-line tool availabe at *http.//www.wipo.int/classification/ipc/en/est/index.html,* associated with the International Patent Classification (IPC) that will facilitate searches for patent information relating to so-called Environmentally Sound Technologies (ESTs) to help in identifying existing and emerging green technologies and potential partners for further R& D and commercial exploitation.

IPC: Training, Electronic Forum and FAQs

The details of Training in the use of IPC are available at http://www.wipo.int/classification/ipc/en/training/index.html.

The International Patent Calssification (IPC) Electronic Forum is available at http://web2.wipo.int/ipc.ief/

Frequently Asked Questions about the IPC are available at *http://www.wipo.int/classifications/ipc/en/faq/index.html.* The first section "General questions related to the IPC" provides answers to questions related to the IPC in general. The second section "Technical questions related to the IPC" answers technical questions related to availability of the IPC, file specifications, standards, etc.

Contact: Send an email to ipc.mail@wipo.int for further information about the IPC

Useful URLs

Strasbourg Agreement
http://www.wipo.int/treaties/en/classification/strasbourg/

International Classification
http://www.wipo.int/classifications/en/

International Patent Classification
http://www.wipo/int/classification/ipc/en/

Nice Classification
http://www.wipo.int/classifications/nice/en/

Locarno Classification
http://www.wipo.int/classifications/locarno/en

Vienna Classification
http://www.wipo.int/classifications/vienna/en/

Cooperative Classification System
http://www.cpcinfo.org/

US Patent Classification System
http://www.uspto.gov/web/patent/classification/

European Patent Classification
http:worldwide.espacenet.com/classification?locale=en_EP

13

WIPO, WTO, UNCTAD & ITC Profiles

Vimal Kumar Varun

World Intellectual Property Organization

http://www.wipo.int, http://www.wipo.org

The World Intellectual Property Organization - referred to in abbreviated form as **WIPO** in English, and **OMPI** in French and Spanish - was established by a convention signed at Stockholm on July 14, 1967, and entitled "Convention Establishing the World Intellectual Property Organization." The WIPO Convention entered into force in 1970. WIPO became a specialized agency in the United Nations system of organizations in 1974 and dedicated to the use of intellectual property (patents, copyright, trademarks, designs, etc.) as a means of stimulating innovation and creativity.

WIPO promote the development and use of the international IP system through Services, Law, Infrastructure and Development.

WIPO works with our member states (http://www.wipo.int/members/en/) and stakeholders to improve understanding and respect for IP worldwide. WIPO provides economic analysis and statistics (http://www.wipo.int/econ_stat/en/) and contribute IP-based solutions to help tackle global challenges (http://www/wipo.int/globalchallenges/en/).

WIPO's nine strategic goals, adopted by WIPO's member states in December 2009 in the first phase of a comprehensive strategic realignment process within the Organization, are given below:

- Balanced Evolution of the International Normative Framework for IP
- Provision of Premier Global IP Services
- Facilitating the Use of IP for Development
- Coordination and Development of Global IP Infrastructure
- World Reference Sources for IP information and Analysis
- International Cooperation on Building Respect for IP
- Addressing IP in Relation to Global Policy Issues
- A Responsive Communications Interface between WIPO, its Member statues and All Stakeholders
- An Efficient administrative and Financial Support Structure to Enable WIPO to deliver its Programs.

They reflect the evolving challenges for WIPO and for intellectual property in today's rapidly changing environment.

The strategic Goals provide the framework for WIPO's six year Medium Term Strategic Plan (2010-2015) http://www.wipo.int/edocs/mdocs/govbody/en/a_48/a_48_3.pdf and for the biennial Program and Budget *http://www.wipo.int/about-wipo/en/budget/.*

The terms governing WIPO's mandate, functions, finances and procedures are set out in the WIPO Convention *(http://www.wipo.int/treaties/en/convention/trtdocs_woO29.html)*

WIPO's member states determine the strategic direction and activities of the Organization. They meet in the Assemblies, committees and working groups (WIPO decision-making bodies).

WIPO's currently have 186 Member States and details are available at http://www.wi po.int/members/en/ and India joined WIPO in 1975. The details related to India are available at http://www.wipo.int/members.en/details.jsp/country_id=80.

The staff of the WIPO Secretariat is drawn from more than 90 countries. They provide the skill and experience to deliver WIPO's diverse services and programs, and to ensure the efficient administration of the Organization.

The respective divisions of the Secretariat are responsible for coordinating the meetings of member states and implementing their decision; for administering the international IP registration systems; for developing and executing the programs designed to achieve WIPO's goals; and for providing a repository of IP expertise to assist its members.

Francis Gurry was appointed as Director General of WIPO on October 1, 2008. He is the fourth Director General of WIPO and his current six-year term runs through September 2014.

The WIPO External Offices serve an important role in bringing WIPO's services and cooperation closer to its member states, stakeholders and partners, and in achieving the Organization's strategic goals. These cover cost-effective support services in respect of the Patent Cooperation Treaty (PCT), Madrid and Hague systems, arbitration and mediation, collective management, research, development, capacity building, and UN system-wide cooperation, in coordination with the relevant sectors in the Headquarters.

Currently WIPO has four offices outside of the Headquarters in Geneva, namely, WIPO Brazil Office (Rio de Janeiro) *http://www.wipo.int.contact/en/area.jsp/area=wbo,* WIPO Japan Offices (Tokyo) *http://www.wipo.int/about-wipo/en/offices/new_york/*, and WIPO Singapore Office *http://www.wipo.int/about-wipo/en/offices/singapore/.*

WIPO IP Services available at *http://www.wipo.int/services/en/* includes Patent (PCT), Trademark (Madrid System), Designs (Hague System), Appellations of Origin (Lisbonn System), Protection of State Emblems (Article 6ter), Arbitration and Meditation Center, Domain Name Dispute Resolution, and International Classification.

The details of Program Activities at WIPO are available at *http://www.wipo.int/activities/en/.* WIPO Resources are available at *http://www.wipo.int/resource/en, WIPO News and Events are available at http.//www.wipo.int/news/en/.*

WIPO maintains an automated system which allows users to subscribe to e-mail notification of news and updates on WIPO's activities, services, events, publications and discussion groups. The specific lists maintained for various areas of interest, with information on available language versions as well as the approximate frequency of notifications are available at http://www.wipo.int/tools/en/mailing-lists/.

The details of treaties administered by WIPO are available at *http://www.wipo.int/treaties/en/ and http://www.wipo.int/wipolex/en/treaties/index_wipo.jsp.*

The details of WIPO Publications are available at *http://www.wipo.int/freepublications/en/.*

Follow WIPO at Facebook (*http:/www.facebook.com/worldipday/*) and Twitter (*http://www.twitter.com/wipo/*)

Contact: World Intellectual Property Organization, 34, Chemin des Colombettes, CH-1211 Geneva 20, Switzerland.

World Trade Organization

http://www.wto.org

The World Trade Organization (WTO) is the only global international organization dealing with the rules of trade between nations. At its heart are the WTO agreements, negotiated and signed by the bulk of the world's trading nations and ratified in their parliaments. The goal is to help producers of goods and services, exporters, and importers conduct their business.

The WTO provides a forum for negotiating agreements aimed at reducing obstacles to international trade and ensuring a level playing field for all, thus contributing to economic growth and development. The WTO also provides a legal and institutional framework for the implementation and monitoring of these agreements, as well as for settling disputes arising from their interpretation and application. The current body of trade agreements comprising the WTO consists of 16 different multilateral agreements (to which all WTO members are parties) and two different plurilateral agreements (to which only some WTO members are parties).

Over the past 60 years, the WTO, which was established in 1995, and its predecessor organization the GATT have helped to create a strong and prosperous international trading system, thereby contributing to unprecedented global economic growth. WTO activities are supported by a Secretariat of some 700 staff, led by the WTO Director-General.

Pascal Lamy is the fifth Director-General of the WTO. His appointment took effect on 1 September 2005 for a four-year term. In April 2009 WTO members reappointed Mr Lamy for a second four-year term, starting on 1 September 2009.

The Secretariat is located in Geneva, Switzerland. The three official languages of the WTI are English, French and Spanish.

The WTO currently has 159 members of which 117 are developing countries or separate customs territories. The details of members and observers are available at *http://www.wto.org/english/thewto_e/whatis_e/tif_e/org6_e.htm.* India joined WTO in 1995. The Member Information of India is available at *http://www/wto.org/english/thewto_e/countries_e/india_e.htm.*

Decisions in the WTO are generally taken by consensus of the entire membership. The highest institutional body is the Ministerial Conference, which meets roughly every two years. A General Council conducts the organization's business in the intervals between Ministerial Conferences. Both of these bodies comprise all members. Specialized subsidiary bodies (Councils, Committees, Sub-Committees), also comprising all members, administer and monitor the implementation by members of the various WTO agreement.

The Main activities of WTO are as follows"

- negotiating the reduction or elimination of obstacles to trade (import tariffs, other barriers to trade) and agreeing on rules governing the conduct of international trade (e.g.antidumping, subsidies, product standards, etc.)
- administering and monitoring the application of the WTO's agreed rules for trade in goods, trade in services, and trade-related intellectual property rights.
- monitoring and reviewing the trade policies of our members, as well as ensuring transparency of regional and bilateral trade agreements.
- settling disputes among our members regarding the interpretation and application of the agreements.
- building capacity of developing country government officials in international trade matters.
- assisting the process of accession of some 30 countries who are not yet members of the organization.
- conducting economic research and collecting and disseminating trade data in support of the WTO's other main activities.
- explaining to and education the public about the WTO, its mission and its activities.

The WTO's founding and guiding principles remain the pursuit of open borders, the guarantee of most-favoured-nation principle and non-discriminatory treatment by and among members, and a commitment to transparency in the conduct of its activities. The opening of national markets to international trade, with justifiable exceptions or with adequate flexibilities, will encourage and contribute to sustainable development, raise people's welfare, reduce poverty, and foster peace and stability. At the same time, such market opening must be accompanied by sound domestic and international policies that contribute to economic growth and development according to each member's needs and aspirations.

WTO's News and Events are available at *http://www/wto.org/english/news_e/statis_e/news_e.htm.*

The WTO's databases and publications provide extensive access to trade and tariff data and details are available at *http:///www.wto.org/english/res_e/statis_e/publications_e/wto_publications_catalogue_2012_e.pdf.*

The WTO's Publication Catalogue is available at *http://www.wto.org/english/res_e/publications_e/wto_publications_catalogue_2012_e.pdf.*

The World Trade Organization E-Learning provides online training on matters related to international trade and WTO Agreements to government officials from developing and least-developed Members and Observers. WTO e-Learning details are available at *http://etraining.wto.org.*

Information on Intellectual Property in WTO, news and official records of the activities of TRIPS Council, and details of the WTO's work with other International Organizations in the field are available at *http://www.wto.org/english/tratop_e/trips_e/trips_e.htm.*

Follow WTO at Facebook (*http://www.facebook.com/worldtradeorganization) and Twitter (http://twitter.com/WTO*)

Contact: World Trade Organization, Centre William Rappard, Rue de Lausanne 154, CH-1211 Geneva 21, Switzerland.

UN Conference on Trade and Development

http://www.unctad.org

UNCTAD, established in 1964, promotes the development-friendly integration of developing countries into the world economy. UNCTAD has progressively evolved into an authoritative knowledge-based institution whose work aims to help shape current policy debates and thinking on development, with a particular focus on ensuring that domestic policies and international action are mutually supportive in bringing about sustainable development.

The organization works to fulfil this mandate by carrying out three key functions.

- It functions as a forum for intergovernmental deliberations, supported by discussions with experts and exchanges of experience, aimed at consensus building.
- It undertakes research, policy analysis and data collection for the debates of government representatives and experts.
- It provides technical assistance tailored to the specific requirements of developing countries, with special attention to the needs of the least developed countries and of economics in transition. When appropriate, UNCTAD co-operates with other organizations and donor countries in the delivery of technical assistance.

The Secretary-General of UNCTAD is Dr. Supachai Panitchpakdi (Thailand), who took office on 1 September 2005.

In performing its functions, the secretariat works together with members Governments and interacts with organizations of the United Nations system and regional commissions, as well as with governmental institutions, non-governmental organizations, the private sector, including trade and industry associations, research institutes and universities worldwide.

The details of member states are given at *http://unctad.org/en/pages/About%20UNCTAD/UNCTAD-Membership.aspx.*

UNCTAD work closely with the organization like World Trade Organization (WTO) International Trade Centre (ITC) and the details are available at *http://unctad.org/en/pages/about%20 UNCTAD/Relationship-with-other-agencies.aspx.*

UNCTADS; s area of work includes Africa. Least Developed Countries and Special Programmes; Globalization and Development; International Trade and Commodities; Investment and Enterprise; Technology and logistics; and details are available at *http://unctad.org/en/pages/Areas_Of_Work.aspx.*

Under its technical cooperation activities, UNCTAD provides assistance tailored to the needs of the developing countries, with special attention being paid to the needs of the least developed countries (LDCs) and countries with the greatest needs. UNCTAD technical cooperation activities are a significant element in achieving the objectives outlined in the Accra Accord adopted by UNCTAD XII, held in Accra (Ghana) in April 2008.

As the focal point within the United Nations system for the integrated treatment of trade and development and interrelated issues in the areas of finance, technology, investment and sustainable development, UNCTAD addresses these issues in a mutually complementary fashion, including through its technical cooperation activities.

UNCTAD technical cooperation is carried out in partnership with other agencies that provide trade-related technical assistance, in consonance with their respective mandates, expertise, and areas of comparative advantage. In delivery of its technical cooperation services, UNCTAD coordinates its activities with its partners, and in particular, members of the United Nation Inter-Agency Cluster on Trade and Productive Capacity.

The United Nations Inter-Agency Cluster on Trade and Productive Capacity was established in 2007 initially as an instrument and platform for contributing to the United Nations system-wide coherence. 1 Since then, it has been converted into a major mechanism for coordination of technical cooperation services provided under the leadership of UNCTAD but its members to developing countries ensuring complementarities, synergies, and sequencing activities.

The thrust of UNCTAD technical coopoeration is human and institutional capacity development in the following main areas of its work, namely:

- Trade policies, trade negotiations and integration of developing countries in the multilateral trading system
- Investment policies and investment promotion and enterprise development
- Trade support services, logistics and trade facilitation
- Special programmes and cross-sectoral issues including Debt Management and Financial Analysis' cross-divisional training programme.

The details of projects under UNCTAD's technical cooperation are available at UNCTAD Technical Cooperation Portal at http://www/unctad.info/en/TC/?mode=AIIProjects

UNCTAD; s publications like Flagship reports, series and policy briefs are available at http://unctad.org/en/pages/media.aspx.

UNCTAD press releases, information notes and resources for journalists are available at *http://unctad.org/en/pages/Media.aspx.*

Follow UNCTAD Twitter (*http://twitter.com/#unctad*)

Contact: UNCTAD, Palais des Nations, 1211 Geneva, Switzerland

International Trade Centre

http://www.intracen.org

The International Trade Centre UNCTAD/WTO (ITC) is the focal point in the United Nations system for technical cooperation with developing countries in trade promotion. ITC was created by the General Agreement on Tariffs and Trade (GATT) in 1964 and since 1968 has been operated jointly by GATT (now by the World Trade Organization, or WTO) and the UN, the latter acting through the United Nations Conference on Trade and Development (UNCTAD). As an executing agency of the United Nations Development Programme (UNDP), ITC is directly responsible for implementing, UNDP- financed projects in developing countries and economics in transition related to trade promotion.

ITC's mission is to foster sustainable economic development and contribute to achieving the Millennium Development Goals in developing countries and countries with economics in transition through trade and international business development. With economics in transition through trade and international business development

ITC's Strategic Objectives are:

— Building awareness and improving the availability and use of trade intelligence

— Strengthening TSIs

— Enhancing policies for the benefit of exporting enterprises

— Building the export capacity of enterprises to respond to market opportunities.

— Mainstream inclusiveness and sustainability into trade promotion and export development policies

ITC's Strategic Plan 2012-2015 is available at http://www.intracen.org/about/strategic-plan/.

ITC is the joint agency of the World Trade Organization and the United Nations.

ITC's aim is for business in developing countries to become more competitive in global market, s speeding economic development and contributing to the achievement of the UN's Millennium Development Goals (MDGs).

Contributing to poverty reduction by boosting trade is a key objective of ITC's trade related technical assistance (TRTA). This is also the focus of the Aid for Trade agenda, which underpins ITCs activities and responds to the developmental needs of the countries we work with.

ITC actively engages the private sector within the multilateral trading system. We are committed to building export success for small and medium sized enterprises (SMEs) in developing and transition countries. We facilitate export development that assures commercial viability of individual companies, empowers women economically, and works towards inclusive economic, social and environmental sustainability.

With more than 40 years of hands-on trade and business experience in the developing world, ITC has a focused approach towards export-led poverty reduction and this is how ITC achieve Export Impact for Goods.

The details of ITC's current projects are available at *http://www.intracen.org/current-projects/.*

ITC is headed by an Executive Director (Ms. Patricia Francis), who reports to the Secretary General of the United Nations Conference on Trade and Development (UNCTAD) and the Director General of the World Trade Organization (WTO). The Senior Management Committed (SMC) is made up the two executive officers and the heads of ITC's four divisions namely Division of Market Development, Division of Country Programmes, Division of Programme Support, and Division of Business and Institutional Support.

Follow ITC at Twitter (*http://twitter.com/ITCnews*)

14

IPR Electronic Journals

Vimal Kumar Varun

Journal of Intellectual Property Rights

Http:/www/niscair.res.in/science communication/Research Journal/rejour/jipr jiprO.asp

Keeping in view the importance of intellectual property rights and their protection, Journal of Intellectual Property Rights (JIPR) was started in 1996. The objective of the journal is enhancing communication between policy makers, organizational agents, academics, and managers on the critical understanding and research on intellectual property; and to promote the development of the newly cultivated research field. The journal publishes contributed/invited articles, case studies and patent reviews; technical notes on current IPR issues; literature review; world literature on IPR; national and international IPR news, book reviews, and conference reports.

JIPR is covered in the abstracting/ indexing services namely Scopus, EBSCO host Electronic Journals Service, Directory of Open Access Journal, Library & Information Science Abstracts database and Legal information Institute of India database.

Contact: Sales and Distribution Officer, National Institute of Science Communication and Information Resources, Dr K S Krishnan Marg (Near Pusa Gate), New Delhi-110012 or write to *sales@niscair.res.in* for subscription details.

International Journal of Intellectual Property Rights

http://www.iaeme.com/IJIPR.asp

The International Journal of Intellectual Property Rights is the authoritative journal for intellectual property questions in relation to trade and investment, with particular focus on the WTO and TRIPS (the Agreement on Trade-Related Aspects of Intellectual Property Rights). More than any other journal, it discusses in depth all TRIPS- related developments, the decisions on TRIPS rendered by the WTO Dispute Settlement Body, and the efforts made by each country to adjust their legislation to TRIPS requirement. However, it also provides much more, and publishes articles by the best experts on a wide range of subjects, such as antitrust and IP rights, encryption, security and privacy in electronic commerce, patents and the copyright exhaustion doctrine, and parallel imports. The international Journal of Intellectual Property Rights is a refereed journal.

The International Journal of Intellectual Property Rights is a quarterly journal focusing on patent rights, copyrights, trademark, trademark law, public interest litigations, WIPO and TRIPS, software and intellectual rights, IPR crimes, remedies and safety, international treaties, conventions and declarations.

Contact: Subscription Manager, International Association of Engineering and Management Education (IAEME), 47, VGP Selva Nagar Extension, Velachery, Chennai-600042 or write to *editor@iaeme.com,* iaemedu @gmail.com for subscription details.

Queen Mary Journal of Intellectual Property

Http://www.e-elgar.com/journals/journal_main.lasso?ref=QMJIP

It is a peer-reviewed academic journal in association with Queen Mary's Intellectual Property Research Institute. The journal aims to foster academic discourse of the highest standard. Published Quarterly the journal will cover the full range of substantive IP topics and deal with both domestic and international issues.

Contact: Marston Book Services Ltd, 160 Eastern Avenue, Milton Park, Abingdon, Oxford shire

OX14 4SB UK or write to *subscriptions@marston.co.uk* for subscription details.

Journal of Intellectual Property Law & Practice

http:/jiplp.oxfortjournals.org

Journal of Intellectual Property Law & Practice (JIPLP), published monthly, is a peer-reviewed journal dedicated to intellectual property law and practice, its coverage includes the full range of substantive IP topics, practice-related matters such as litigation, enforcement, drafting and transactions, plus relevant aspects of related subjects such as competition and world trade law.

The journal is specifically designed for IP lawyers, patent attorneys and trade mark attorneys both in private practice and working in industry. It also aims to be an essential source of reference for academics specializing in IP, members of the judiciary, officials in IP registries and regulatory bodies, and institutional libraries, Subject-matter covered is chosen for its practical relevance and international interest.

Contact: Customer Service Centres based on UK, USA and Japan at the details given on *http://www.oxfordjournals.org/contact_us.html.*

Journal of Intellectual Property, Information Technology and E-Commerce Law

http://www.jipitec.eu

Journal of Intellectual Property, Information Technology and E-Commerce Law (JIPITEC) is a new Online-Journal for current issues of intellectual property, information technology and E-commerce law. The main focus on JIPTEC is on European law – both on the EU-level and on the member states-level. Most articles are in English language, but the journal is also open for articles in other European languages, especially German and French.

JIPITEC is an Open Access Journal Articles are available according to the terms and conditions of the Digital Peer Publishing Licenses (http://www.dipp.nrw.de/lizenzen/. In addition, authors may permit the use of their articles under a Creative Commons *(http://creativecommons.org/about/licenses/)* or other license.

JIPITEC is a peer-reviewed journal. Submissions to the editors are welcome and will be processed according to the peer review guidelines within 4 weeks. Its articles may be downloaded and used everywhere and without fees.

Contact: Details are available at *http://www/jipitec.eu/about-the-journal/contact.*

Texas Intellectual Property Law Journal

http://www/utexas.edu/law/journals/tiplj/

TIPLJ is a leading intellectual property law journal, and we strive to be the forum of choice for intellectual property law practitioners, professors, and students around the globe. Our primary focus centers on providing significant and innovative contributions to U.S. and international intellectual property law. We are sponsored by the IP section of the State Bar of Texas. We have the largest subscription base of all law journals published through The University of Texas, and we provide positive revenue to UT through publication royalties.

Articles appearing in the Journal focus on cutting edge. Substantive legal issues and recent developments of interest to our practitioner and academic subscribers in the areas of Patent, Copyright, Trademark, Unfair Competition, and Trade

Secret law, as well as other areas of law in the context of IP (e.g. constitutional , contracts, antitrust, criminal, torts, international M & A, corporate, administrative law). TIPLJ also publishes articles concerning issues arising in IP litigation and practice before the U.S. Patent and Trademark Office, state and federal courts. Articles submitted for publication in the Journal are written by academicians, practitioners, and students from around the world.

Contact: Send on email to *tiplj@tiplj.org* for General Inquiries and send an email to *publications@law.utexas.edu* for Subscription details.

Journal of Intellectual Property Law

http://www.law.uga.edu/jipl/

The Journal of Intellectual Property Law was founded in 1993 University of Georgia School of Law and is the nation's oldest student-edited law journal devoted exclusively to the field of intellectual property law. This journal is run by the students at the University of Georgia School of Law and publishes two volumes each year (Fall & Sprint) with articles by leading scholars, judges, practicing attorneys, and students that address the constantly changing subject areas of trade secrets, patent law, trademarks, copyrights, Internet law, and entertainment & sports law.

Contact: Send an email with name and address to *jipl@uga.edu* for subscription details.

IP WIRE

http://www.ipwire.com

IP Wire is the only newsletter dedicated solely on IP Deals, IP Tech Transfer, and IP Commercialization transactions.

Contact: Send an email to *info@ipwire.com* for more information

Intellectual Property Today

http://www.iptoday.com

Intellectual Property Today, published monthly since 1994, focuses on legal issues in patent, trademark and copyright law. Content is geared to the patent attorneys and agents, professionals and executives in firms and companies that provide products and services to this industry. Features emphasize developments in cutting edge technology and their effect on intellectual property law practice.

Contact: Intellectual Property Today at *planet@iptoday.com* for more details.

The Intellectual Property & Technology Forum & Journal

http://bciptf.org

The Intellectual Property & Technology Forum & Journal at Boston College Law School is a legal publication dedicated to providing readers with rigorous, innovative scholarship, timely reporting, and ongoing discussion from the legal community concerning technology law and intellectual property. The Forum is designed edited and published by students at Boston College Law School. Our articles are available freely on this web site at *http://bciptf.org./category/articles/.*

The PTO Bulletin

http://www/uspto.gov/web/office/ac/ahrpa/opa/bulletin/index.html

USPTO's Office of Public Affairs publishes frequent news updated containing interesting and important information about issues affecting the Patent and Trademark Office. This communiqué is called: the pto bulletin. The editor of the pto bulletin welcomes your comments at *brigid.guinn@uspto.gov.*

EPO-Patent Information News

http:/www.epo.org/service-support/publications/patent-information/news.html

Patent Information News is a quarterly publication that informs European patent information users of new developments in the area.

To receive an e-mail notification when a new edition of Patent information News is published please use the subscription form at *http://forms.epo.org./service-support/publications/pi-news-form-html.*

15

Patent Writing: An Approach with Example

S.M.Mathur and Priti Mathur

A Patent is a written document explaining an invention with exclusive right. It is used to protect an inventor/scientist and to prevent other from making profits without permission. It is also used as an authority paper permitting license holders to duplicate the results. A patent application requires a combination of legal documentation and technical papers. This issue makes patent writing a very different writing style.

In India, patent applications can be filed by a patent agent or an individual having some scientific and technical background to understand the invention. However, no one can understand the invention better than the inventors themselves. Document preparation requires healthy discussions between the inventor and agent. For inventors, a good understanding on patent writing style can greatly facilitate the documentation process. Before filing the patent application inventor must be sure about that the subject is eligible for patent protection, the invention has something new, the invention is not obvious and is not easily predictable from general consensus, and the invention has practical application.

A typical patent application includes the following sections:
Title
Description of field of the invention
Background of the invention
Summary of the invention
Brief description of the drawings
Detailed description
Examples if any
Claims
Abstract

The patent title should be short as much as possible. Using new or difficult words will create problems in a patent search. For example, if a patent is related to an agricultural implement, then it is better to use name of the implement, rather than a soil working tool. The patent title and names of the inventors' should be on a separate page. The field of invention is used to specify its major applications in the field. The background of the invention should include brief information of the invention's application, the present status, relevant patents in the field, and the details of drawbacks to be overcome. It is difficult to give the details of all relevant patents in the application but the patent which very closely matches with the invention should be included and the difference between the existing technology and the new invention must be highlighted. These discussions should be in sequence in a way to make it obvious that the present application is able to make a substantial increment on its final product and is noticeably different from prior arts. The process should be explained with flow diagram or drawings. A detailed description of drawings provides a clear picture of the invention. Examples are to be given to illustrate different embodiments of the inventions. The purpose is to explain the feasibility of the invention and improvements from prior arts. Details should be given in a way that the results can be reproduced by an expert in the field.

The summary of the invention should be in one paragraph to briefly explain the invention. The summery should include the major purpose of the invention. It includes concentrated information about a detailed description and claims. In case of invention of a machine, the range of independent variables and selected parameters should also be mentioned.

Claims are to be formed very carefully as it is the heart of a patent document. It should cover all new results/concepts mentioned in inventions. Claims should always be numbered. The first claim should be as general as possible. Inventor should be very clear about the dependent or independent claims. One should not hesitate to take the help of an expert or study the similar patents before writing claims.

For university teachers or persons working with some organizations has to follow certain procedures to finalize a patent. The most important part will be financing the first step is submitting a disclosure to the authority or in big institutes to the division of technology transfer and commercialization. The disclosure can be written as lab notes or technical papers. Once disclosure is approved, patent agents hired by the university will work with inventors to draft the patent application. It is often preferred to file a provisional patent application before filing a formal patent application. One big advantage of filing a provisional application is allowing universities to have more time for market evaluation and commercialization. If no company expresses the interest to license the technique, universities have the option to convert it to a full application or to abandon it. In some of the universities the patent cells are not available and a scientist has to search his own sources. In such cases TIFAC, New Delhi has a patent cell which provide help to scientist to file a patent application through them. TIFAC will examine the subject at their level and if found suitable they will provide a patent attorney who will draft the patent application and prepare all technical and legal documents. The biggest advantages are that the TIFAC will bear all the expenses of patent filling as well as charges of patent attorney.

Important things to be remembered

- Before filling a patent application one must be sure that the subject is eligible for patent protection, the invention should have something new, the invention is not obvious and is not easily predictable from general consensus and invention has practical application and commercial viability.
- Do not make your invention public before filing a patent application. If you make it public by demonstration article in a journal or newspaper, publicity by mouth, advertisement, or any other way-before you apply for a patent, you are making your invention public. This could mean that you lose the possibility of being granted a patent.
- If inventor needs to talk to some business partners he should ask them to sign a non-disclosure agreement. The language of the agreement can be prepared by any legal advisor or patent agent.
- Inventor or inventors can prepare a patent document themselves by seeing some previously filed patent documents or with the help of this book. But in case of any difficulty you should consult a patent agent as he will take less time for preparation of document and will formulate the claims in a legal way. Patent attorneys are legally qualified and some will give you initial advice free of charge. There are other patent advisers, consultants and inventor-support organizations that may also be able to help or advise you. We are not allowed to recommend any particular patent attorney or other adviser. However a list of patent attorneys is available on internet.

Table 1: Comparison chart of Patents

Patent No.	CN 2857449 (Y)	CN2715488 (Y)	JP2002095344 (A)	KR 200170455 (Y1)	CN2383303 (Y)	Present Invention
Patent Title	Machine for Crushing Stubble and leaving Same in field	Dry field clod crushing and weed eradication machine for intertill	Hopper and reaped weed-crushing device of reaped weed-crushing machine	Cutting machine for cutting or crushing weed or tree branches	Weed Breaker	A mechanical system for chopping and crushing of water hyacinth
Inventor(s)	YIN SHAOJUN	MAGUOFA OGUMA YUKIO	KONDO KEIJI; LI JINGBO; LIU ZHEN	LEEHEE-YOUNG	JIAZHENGUANG;	S.M.Mathur
Salient Features system	• It is a soil working machine • Used for crushing the stubbles in the field • Gearbox and clutch assembly • It has a cutter only not the adjustable blades • Work for dry stubble only • It will not deal With the complete • Plant specially having bulb and high moisture	• It is a soil working machine • Used for crushing the weeds and dry clods in the field • It is just like a plow used for tillage operations • It has spike teeth for steering the soil not the cutting blades and crushing system • It is basically a farm machine which is used for	• Used for dried long weeds • A different system to hopper is provided to feed the weeds • Not suitable for green weeds having high moisture content • It will not deal with the complete plant specially having bulb and high moisture content	Not available	• It is a multifunctional machine • Soil working element has to be removed before using a cutting or crushing weed or tree branches • Knifes are mounted on a rotating shaft • Machine is used for terrace cultivation orchards and greenhouse • It will not dealt with the complete plant specially having bulb	• This invention relates to a mechanical for chopping and crushing of water hyacinth in a single pass in the machine • Hopper consisted of a cutting cylinder and a shear plate with 36 nos of adjustable blades mounted on cutting cylinder • No. Of blades can

Patent No.	CN 2857449 (Y)	CN2715488 (Y)	JP2002095344 (A)	KR 200170455 (Y1)	CN2383303 (Y)	Present Invention
Patent Title	Machine for Crushing Stubble and leaving Same in field	Dry field clod crushing and weed eradication machine for intertill	Hopper and reaped weed-crushing device of reaped weed-crushing machine	Cutting machine for cutting or crushing weed or tree branches	Weed Breaker	A mechanical system for chopping and crushing of water yacinth
Inventor(s)	YIN SHAOJUN	MAGUOFA OGUMA YUKIO	KONDO KEIJI; LI JINGBO; LIU ZHEN	LEEHEE-YOUNG	JIAZHENGUANG;	S.M.Mathur
	Content • Single cutting Knife is used and Fixed at the end of output shaft • It is a machine cutting stublles after harvesting a crop • The cut and crushes stubbles are left into the filed for decomposition	land preparation in the field • It will not deal with the complete plant specially having bulb and high moisture content • It is a machine mainly used for inter culture operation before or after sowing • It has spikes as A crushing element			and high moisture content	be varied between 12-36 • Machine is having two corrugated pressing rollers to reduce the moisture content of the cut material • Machine is capable of breaking the bulb of water hyacinth • Capable of reducing weight and volume both in single operation

In order to understand the above mentioned points clearly please go through an application filed for the patent. The presented case is a typical example of scientist who has developed a new machine and was interested in filling a patent application. Scientist approached to TIFAC, New Delhi and after studying the details of newly developed machine and search they have allotted a patent attorney to scientist. A meeting was held between attorney and scientist and he briefed about the invention to the attorney. The rough draft was prepared by the scientist himself and finally refined by the patent attorney before filling it to the patent office. The filling was done only after the draft was approved by the inventor.

The Example of Preparation of a patent draft/application is as follows

The Patents Act, 1970

Complete specification

Section 10

Title

" A Mechanical System for Chopping and Crushing of Water Hyacinth"

Applicant

Indian Council of Agricultural Research, Krishi Bhavan, Dr. Rajendra Prasad Road, New Delhi-110 001

The following specification particularly describes the invention and the manner in which it is to be performed.

FIELD OF INVENTION

This invention relates to a mechanical system for chopping and crushing of water hyacinth

Prior Art:

Water hyacinth [Eichhornia crassipes (Mart.) Solms] is the most predominant persistent and troublesome aquatic weed in the world and has posed ecological and economical problems in several countries. Utilization of water hyacinth as animal feed, as a fuel, handicrafts, furniture, biogas, compost, pollution abatement and paper pulp has been done. However, one of the major problems faced was bulk and the cost of transportation of freshly harvested water hyacinth from water bodies to the factories. Hence the major objectives were to determine the physical and bulk mechanical properties of water hyacinth and to evaluate the suitability of available choppers/crushers for water hyacinth.

The matured water hyacinth plant (Eichhornia crassipes) consists of long, fibrous roots which may be up to three meters in length, rhizomes, buoyant petioles, stolons, leaves, inflorescence and fruit clusters. The petioles are the leaf stems and the stolons are the runners, which form new plants. The inflorescence bears between 6 and 120 lily like violet and yellow flowers most commonly between 8 and 15. Like most flowers, which are at their best when the soil is impoverished, water hyacinth has the best flowers when the nutrients in water are in short supply. The fruit is a capsule, containing up to 450 seeds. Altogether, the plant can grow up to a meter high. Water hyacinth plant has shiny dark green leaves. Water hyacinths grow over wide variety of wetland types from lakes, streams, ponds, waterways, ditches, and backwater areas.

This free floating fresh water plant has spread from tropical South America to at least fifty countries around the world. The plant originated in the rich and diverse rain forests of the Amazon River. Basin and was introduced into many parts of the world as an ornamental garden pond plant owing to its beauty in India it was first introduced as on ornamental plant in 1896 from Brazil (Aquaphyte, 2001). It spreads over 5,00,000 hectares of water among the states of Andhra Pradesh, Uttar Pradesh, Tamil Nadu, West Bengal, Rajasthan and Orissa. In India, water hyacinth is known by different names such as Jalkumbhi, Falkumbi, Shokh Samunder (Hindi), Pisachi Thanana (Tamil), Kachuripuri (Bengali) and Kulavali (Kannada). It is particularly suited to tropical and sub tropical countries where environmental conditions favour a year round growing period and has become a problem plant in areas of Southern USA, South America, East, West & Southern Africa, South-East Asia and Australia. The capacity of water hyacinth to grow and reproduce is phenomenal and in one growing season 25 plants can give rise to 2 million plants, covering one hact. And weight is much as a fully loaded Jumbo Jet (Lindsey and Hirt, 1999). The natural loss of water from the water surface by evaporation is thought to increase through transpiration from the leaves of water hyacinth by at least 40 to 50 per cent (Lindsey and Hirt 1999). Due to this, sometimes it is called “Shokh Samunder” in India. The oxygen depleting load of one hact. Of water hyacinth mat is equivalent to the sewage created by 80 persons (Gopal and Sharma, 1981). This action lowers the natural ability of water body to absorb organic pollution and create septic and odorous conditions. Over the years, various control methods have been studied and tried including chemical, biological and mechanical means but with no lasting success. It is effective and relatively cheaper than the mechanical and manual control. However, their long-term effects on the environment are unknown and sprayed plants were left to rot in the water causing pollution and aggravated entrophication. The plants cannot be completely controlled by biological method. Control by mechanical and manual harvesting has been widely practiced in many countries. The simplest mechanical method of control would be to chop the water hyacinth in situ and leave it to rot in the water. This however, has two main drawbacks:

- The plant is wasted (not utilized)
- In the process of decay, the chopped plant extracts oxygen from the water causing suffocation to animal life in water body.

A major contributory factor to the failure of water hyacinth machinery is the large volume and moisture content of water hyacinth, which slows down the harvesting operation by increasing requirement for handling, transport and cut down harvester productivity with increased harvesting cost. It also limits effective utilization due to low dry matter content and high drying equipment costs. Water hyacinth removed in large quantities from water body can be transported easily when chopped and crushed to higher densities. Packaging to higher density than the conventional bale reduce the problem of transportation, storage space and provides better flow characteristics during material handing (Ferrero et al. 1999). Chopping and compressing or compacting has been proposed as means of reducing volume and weight or increasing density (Stewarts, 1972; Cifuentes, 1976: Bagnall 1980 and 1982). Chopping and compacting have been proposed as means of reducing volume or increasing density for easy handling and transportation of forage plants (Ferrero et al.1991). Generally flail, flywheel and cylindrical types of choppers are used for forage chopping (Bernaki et al. 1972) stated that in a flail type forage chopper, the accuracy of chopping was worse for cutting fresh corn stalks. Bernaki also studied on flywheel chopper and cylindrical chopper and finally concluded that the cylindrical chopper was in many respects functionally better than flywheel one. Kanafojski and Karwowski (1976) studied the energetic of knife-type choppers. It was also concluded that the power requirement for a cylindrical type chopper was approximately 7 percent lower in case of flywheel type chopper under identical working conditions. Bangall (1982) worked on fresh water hyacinth and he reported that compression to 400 Kg/m^3 required 2.4-watt-h/t and 800 Kg/m^3 required 7.8 watt-h/t energy respectively. O'Dougherty (1982) concluded that the blades used in forage chopping should have a blade angle in the range of 30^0 to 40^0 with a rake angle of 10 to 20^0 cutting up to speeds of 30 m/s. The review shows that the power loss due to the water resistance and mechanical losses were high in flail type of cutters and also the accuracy of cutting was worse.

Crushing and pressing of plants is one of the commonly used methods for expressing appreciable amount of plants juice (Calilung 1990). However, several investigators have explored more intensive crushing of alfalfa and other forage crops (Chancellor, 1955, 1964 and Spencer et al., 1969). Under intensive crushing treatments. 50 per cent of the initial moisture and an appreciable amount of the soluble dry matter may be removed from the harvested material as the liquid fraction. Rollers, piston extrusion, cone press and screw presses are the most commonly used equipments used for crushing of fibrous agricultural products. The power requirement for a cylinder type of chopper is approximately 7 percent lower than in case of flywheel type chopper under identical conditions. Therefore, cylindrical choppers can be selected for chopping of water hyacinth for volume reduction over conventional flail and fly wheel types of choppers. The review also suggested that chopping the biomass reduction are two separate processes. The review indicated that the most attractive alternation for solving the water hyacinth problem is integrated harvesting and utilization, which offers potential benefits in terms of generation of useful products (AQUAPHYTE, 2001: Mathur et al. 2003). The mechanical mean is the only safe and rapid method to control the growth of water hyacinth but the disposal costs are high because of its bulk. In order to solve this problem, water hyacinth has to be chopped and crushed. The chopped and crushed plants will not allow water hyacinth to re-grow.

US 5,487, 258 discloses

A system for the harvest of water hyacinths. The floating hyacinths are conveyed from their surface disposed growing disposition to a grinder. Grinding occurs with liberation of large amount of the plant contained water and exposure of the hyacinths' fibrous plant material which only becomes suitable for baling after grinding has occurred. Thereafter, the hyacinths; fibrous material is placed into a conventional baler where the now ground plant material adheres when baled into a cohesive mass. The baled fibrous material is then disposed of. For example, the baled material can be attached to rope, and pushed into the water with bales being serially attached one to another via the rope. One end of the rope is led ashore. Thereafter, the serially tethered bales are pulled floating from harvesting barge to a shore location where conventional removal of the compacted and abled fibrous biomass can occur. In one embodiment, the bales are further compacted on the shore before transport for fuel or other uses. In another embodiment, a shore mounted facility accumulates, grinds and bales the water hyacinth. Weighting of the bales for disposal by sinking is disclosed.

CN 1544165 discloses

A ship-carried Eichhornia crassipes solm automatic dehydrator, composed of salvage and transportation system, dehydrating system and purifying system. The salvage is completed by salvage and transportation system, and it can implement extensive-depth salvage procedure by depth adjusting rod. The hole conveyer belt can eliminate most adhesive water in the transporting course. The dehydrating system can meet the dehydrating requirements at different degrees by roller adjusting rod. The emersion water can achieve national land water effluent stand through many layers of different-aperture nylon filter net and sand filter, implement discharging without pollution.

US 5, 603, 204 discloses

Floating aquatic vegetation harvested from the surface of a body of water. The vegetation is chopped or shredded when floating in situ on the body of water. The vegetation is then removed from the water surface. The chopping, shredding, tearing or other action breaks down the structure of the plants or subdivides them into smaller parts. This reduces the structure of the plant and allows it to be compacted to a much higher density mass so that it can be handled more readily. The apparatus for harvesting the vegetation includes a self- propelled vessel. A shredding head is carried on the vessel for shredding the vegetation as the platform advances theracross and removing the shredded vegetation form the surface of the body of water. The vegetation shredding means are two rotors arranged in a shallow V arrangement across the front end of the vessel, with the point of V directed forwardly, in the direction of travel. Rotors arranged in this way assist with the positive tracking of the platform. When rotated so that the bottom of the rotor travels towards the rear, and the top towards the front, the vegetation is directed towards the center of the vessel, behind the rotors, in a windrow for subsequent pickup. The V configurations also limits dispersion of the vegetation around the ends of the rotors. The rotors are covered on the top and ends by a shroud. This assists in preventing dispersal of the rent material and serves as part of the collecting system.

The above cited documents deal with the water hyacinth till the harvesting.

Further, it is known to have a provision for dumping of chopped hyacinth at the lake shore, which leads to formation of a heap. This causes environmental pollution as the chopped plants extract oxygen from water affecting adversely animal lives. Further, in case of suitable ground condition i.e. muddy or watery ground, the chopped plants can regrow. Yet further, due to large volume of the plants, transportation of the same is expensive.

Further, a device is known to have been provided in the art which comprises a boat loaded with a grinder to grind the plants collected from the water surface to a paste, from which water can't be separated.

The disadvantage associated with the above is that, water becomes unsuitable to drink upon getting mixed again with the lake (after release from grinding of water hyacinth).

The chopped plants can be crushed by a screw conveyor. However, the same is associated with several disadvantages as listed below:

i. It is time dependent i.e. it consumes a lot of time.
ii. Crushed water hyacinth causes chocking of holes and outlets of the barrel of the screw.
iii. The plants travel a long distance, which causes chocking of fibrous roots in the barrel hole and at the out let of the screw auger.

In cylinder type chopper, chopping may be effective but crushing can't be coupled with screw auger which requires forced feeding and having low capacity and does not match with the chopping speed of the cutting cylinders causing a bridging effect at the inlet of the screw.

OBJECTS OF THE INVENTION

An object of the present invention is to propose a system for chopping and crushing of water hyacinth which is installed at the shore or on the harvester form which crushed plants can be taken to site for reuse.

Another object of the present invention is to propose a system for chopping and crushing of water hyacinth which prevents regrowth of the plants.

Further object of the present invention is to propose a system for chopping and crushing of water hyacinth reduce volume of the plant by 65-70% resulting in reduction of cost for transportation.

Still another object of the present invention is to propose a system for chopping and crushing of water hyacinth which can be reused for various applications.

Yet another object of the present invention is to propose a system for chopping and crushing of water hyacinth which does not cause environmental pollution.

Still another further object of the present invention is to propose a system for chopping the crushing of water hyacinth which is cost effective and efficient.

Yet further object of the present invention is to propose a system for chopping and crushing of water hyacinth which consumes less in put power.

Further object of the present invention is to propose as system for chopping and crushing of water hyacinth which is simple in construction.

Still another object of the present invention is to propose a system for chopping and crushing of water hyacinth which deals with the plants after harvesting of the same.

Another object of the present invention is to propose a system for chopping and crushing of water hyacinth which is easy to operate.

Yet another object of the present invention is to propose a system for chopping and crushing of water hyacinth which can be mounted on boat harvester.

Further another object of the present invention is to propose a system for chopping and crushing of water hyacinth which can be automatic and is having high capacity.

STATEMENT OF INVENTIAON

According to this invention there is provided a mechanical system for chopping and crushing of water hyacinth comprises a frame accommodating a hopper disposed with a cutting cylinder and a shear plate at its bottom for cutting the plants, a crushing cylinder and a pressing roller provided under the hopper for crushing of the plants and a delivery conveyor for delivery of the chopped and crushed plants to a transporting unit.

BRIEF DESCRIPTION OF THE ACCOMPANYING DRAWING

Further objects and advantages of this invention will be more apparent from the ensuring description when read in conjunction with the accompanying drawing and wherein:

DETAILED DESCRIPTION OF THE INVENTION WITH REFERENCE TO THE ACCOMPANYING DRAWING

The system of present invention as shown in fig.1 may comprise a conveyor system to transport the Hyacinth plants to a main hopper (1). The conveyor or system comprises a hopper (22) to admit plants therein. A conveyor belt (10) is provided between two rollers (8 and 9) to deliver the plants into the main hopper (1). Further, the conveyor system comprises a chain and sprocket system (19) as shown in figure connected to the roller (9) to drive the same. The sprocket (19) is connected to a D.C.motor (20) as the speed of the conveyor system is required to be maintained at low level. The main hopper (1) is provided as its bottom with a cutting roller (2) and a sheer plate (3) maintained at a clearance from each other. A pressing and crushing roller (6 and 5) are provided below the cutting roller (2) for crushing and chopped plants falling from above. Thereafter, chopped and crushed material is delivered to a transporting unit by means of a delivery conveyer (8-10, 15 and 16) disposed below the crushing and pressing roller. The rollers (9) is provided with an adjusting screw (7) to control the tension in the conveyor belt (10 if required. The driving to the rollers is provided by prime mover (11) provided at the bottom. All the above roller, hopper etc are mounted on a frame, to which the conveyor system is detachably fixed.

The details of different components of the system are as follows:

Hopper: The hopper is trapezoidal in shape provided with slot in both the side walls and rear wall to facilitate fitting of shear plate (3) against the cutting cylinder (2).

Cutting Cylinder with Blades: The cutting cylinder (2) is provided with at least a set of rings, one at each end of the cylinder detachably mounted with plurality of blades by means of connecting pieces such as square pieces fixedly held to the ring. Further, a circular plate is provided at each end of the cylinder so as to cover the same. The shear plate (3) is fixedly provided against the rotating cylinder to act as counter cutting edge. The blade and shear plate are preferably made of spring steel for longer life wherein the number of blades can be varied from 12-36 preferably 36.

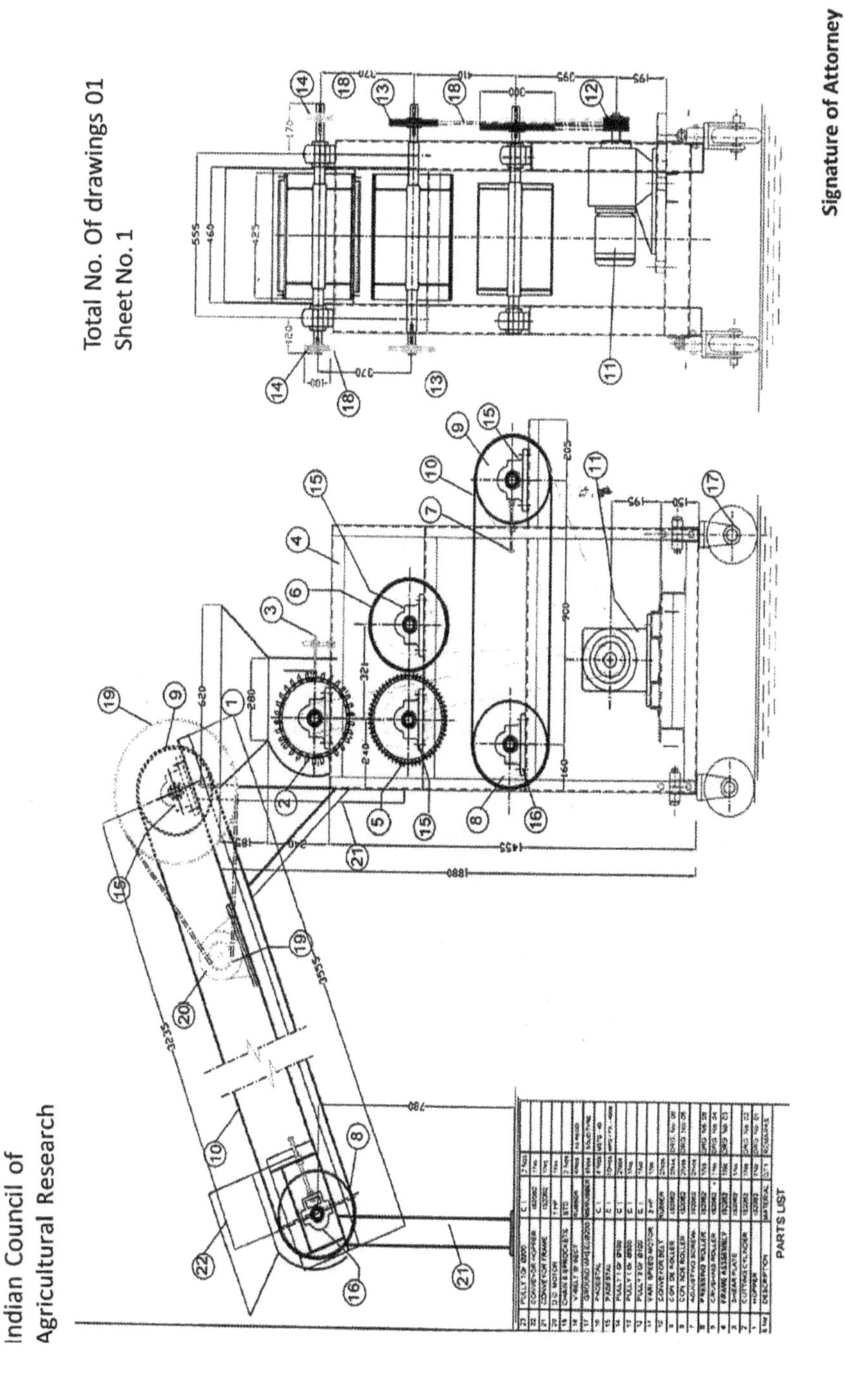
Indian Council of
Agricultural Research
Total No. Of drawings 01
Sheet No. 1
Signature of Attorney
PARTS LIST

Crushing Roller: The crushing roller is provided with a plurality of uniformity distributed corrugations on its periphery for providing positive thrust to flow the chopped material and welded with a plate at each end.

Pressing Roller: The pressing roller is disposed with a rubber lining throughout its outer surface rotating against the crushing roller in opposite direction for crushing of chopped material. Provision of rubber lining is made to avoid noise pollution. This roller is also covered by a plate at each end like other. The prime mover (11) drives all the rollers and delivery conveyor through suitable pulleys and v-belts. The DC motor is used to drive the feeding conveyor through chain and sprockets to get a speed ratio of for example 1:6.

The electric power required for chopping and crushing increases with the increase in flow rate and speeds of cutting cylinder and crushing roller. The system of the present invention is capable of chopping and crushing the plants in a single pass. The system is covered with safety covers to avoid any accident. The chopped and crushed water hyacinth can be used as animal feed, mulch, compost, a source of pulp for making paper and board, rope, crafts, furniture, fuel, a medicinal plant and pollution abatement. The system also allows removal of surface and free cell water.

It is to be noted that the present invention is susceptible to modifications, adaptation and changes by those skilled in the art. Such variant embodiments employing the concepts and features of this invention are intended to be within the scope of the present invention, which is further set forth under the following claims:-

We Claim

1. A mechanical system for chopping and crushing of water hyacinth comprises a frame accommodations a hopper (22) disposed with a cutting cylinder (2) and a shear plate (3) at its bottom for cutting the plants, a crushing cylinder and a pressing roller provided under the hopper (22) for crushing of the plants and a delivery conveyor or belt (10) for delivery of the chopped and crushed plants to a transporting unit.
2. A mechanical system as claimed in claim 1 wherein the said system provided with a conveyor system such as herein described for delivering of the plants into the hopper.
3. A mechanical system as claimed in claim 1 or 2 wherein the said hopper (22) is provided with slot on side and rear walls with a shear plate (3) fitted therein.
4. A mechanical system as claimed in any of the preceding claims wherein the cutting cylinder (2) is provided with at least one ring at its each end detachably disposed with a plurality of blades by means of a connecting means fixedly held to the ring.

5. A mechanical system as claimed in claim 4 wherein the blades are 12-36 in number preferably 36.
6. A mechanical system as claimed in any of the preceding claims wherein the cutting cylinder (2) and shear plate (3) are provided with a clearance there between.
7. A mechanical system as claimed in any of the preceding claims wherein the crushing cylinder is provided with uniformly distributed corrugations throughout its surface
8. A mechanical system as claimed in any of the preceding claims wherein the pressing roller (5 & 6) is provided with a rubber lining throughout its outer surface rotating against the crushing cylinder in opposite direction.
9. A mechanical system as claimed in any of the preceding claims wherein the delivery convey or (8-10, 15 and 16) comprises a belt (10) around two rollers (8 & 9) with an adjusting screw (7) disposed with one of the rollers.
10. A mechanical system as claimed in any of the preceding claims comprising a prime mover (11) to drive the rollers (8 & 9) and conveyor mounted on the frame and a D.C. Motor (20) for driving the conveyor system.

Abstract

"A mechanical system for chopping and crushing of water hyacinth". This invention relates to a mechanical system for chopping and crushing of water hyacinth in a single machine comprises a frame accommodating a hopper disposed with a cutting cylinder and a shear plate at its bottom for cutting the plants, a crushing cylinder and a pressing roller provided under the hopper for crushing of the plants and a delivery conveyor for delivery of the chopped and crushed plants to transporting unit. The system is capable of chopping and crushing of water hyacinth in a single pass and reduces the volume up to 65-70 percent and cost of transportation (Fig 1).

APPLICANTS ATTORNEY

After the submission of the patent application it will be published after a certain period of time. The time limits, various application forms, fee and definitions of various terms can be been seen on Indian patent site at *www.ip**india**.nic.in/ or for more details one can see the ip**india**.nic.in/**ipr**/patent/Draft Patent_**Manual**_2008.pdf. The manual is very helpful and it also contains the detailed procedure for e-filling of patent application. For intellectuals or patent agents e-filling is very easy and one has to get the digital signature and register for e-filling. To discuss the process of e-filling is beyond the scope of this paper but for details one can see the www.ip**india**.nic.in/**ipr**/patent/ DraftPatent_**Manual**_2008.pdf.*

After publication the patent application will go for the examination. The report of examination will be send to the applicant or a patent attorney with a time limit. One has to remove all the objections or clarify the various points raised by the examiner. In the said example examiner raised some of the issues and the same was communicated to inventor through attorney.

Patent attorney asked inventor that regarding objection1, the controller states that the present invention is anticipated by CN 2857449, CN 2715488, JP 2002095344, KR 200170455 and CN 2383303. Kindly provide with the novelty of present invention over cited documents.

Regarding objection 2 and 3, attorney have amended the claims.

Rest of the objections were formal in nature and were being taken care by attorney at the time of filling the response.

Inventor studies the objection 1 carefully and presented a comparative chart mentioning the novelty of the developed machine as shown in table 1.

The main difference among above mentioned patents and the present innovation is that all other patents are related to Farm Machinery and multifunctional machine. Whereas; the water hyacinth chopper cum crusher does not have any soil working tool as compare to patent CN 2857449 (Y), CN 2715488 (Y), JP 2002095344 (A) and CN 2383303 (Y). Water hyacinth is a special type of aquatic plant having moisture content of more than 90 per cent and a bulb at the root. In order to destroy the plant this bulb has to be cust and crushed completely. Special care was taken in this machine to crush the bulb completely. The plant has to pass first between a cutting cylinder and a shear plate than two corrugated rollers which will crush the bulb completely. In the above mentioned patents no machine has this mechanism and machines are used to cut or crush the dry stubble or weeds. Water hyacinth chopper can be used on the boat or on the site of a river or lakes where as above mentioned machines have to be used in the fields only. The above table clearly shows the difference among the patents.

The novelty of the machine is that cutting and crushing both the operation can be done in a single pass in a single machine with two different mechanisms thus weight and volume of the plant will reduce to 60-65 and 35-40 per cent respectively. The bulb of the plant will destroyed completely which will not allow plant to regrow. Freshly harvested plant can be chopped immediately.

Attorney redrafted the claims as under

We claim

1. A Mechanical system for chopping of water hyacinth plants comprises a conveyor system accommodating a hopper (22) disposed with the cutting roller (2) and a shear plate (3) at its bottom for cutting the plants,

characterized by crushing roller and a pressing roller provided under the hopper (22) for crushing of the plants and a delivery conveyor belt (10) for delivery of the chopped and crushed plants to a transporting unit.

2. A Mechanical system as claimed in any of the preceding claims, wherein the cutting roller (2) is provided with at least one ring at its each and detachable disposed with a plurality of blades by means of a connecting means fixedly held to the ring.
3. A Mechanical system as claimed in claim 2, wherein the blades are 12-36 in number, preferably 36.
4. A Mechanical system as claimed in any of the preceding claims, wherein the cutting roller is (2) and shear plate (3) are provided with a clearance there between
5. A Mechanical system as claimed in any of the preceding claims, wherein the crushing roller is provided with uniformly distributed corrugations______its surface.
6. A Mechanical system as claimed in any of the preceding claims, wherein the pressing roller (5,6) is provided with a rubber lining throughout its outer surface rotating against the crushing roller in opposite direction.
7. A Mechanical system as claimed in any of the preceding claims, wherein the delivery conveyor or belt (8, 10, 15 and 16) is provided between two rollers (8, 9) with an adjusting screw (7) disposed with roller (9).
8. A Mechanical system as claimed in any of the preceding claims comprising prime mover (11) for driving the rollers (8,9)

By this way the objections were waved off. Finally the patent was granted with patent number off 255661

References

Aquaphyte, 2001. A News Letter Published by Center for Aquatic and Invasive plants, Gainesville, Florida. Vol. 21, Number 2, Winter 2001, ISSN-0893-7702

Bagnall, L.O.1980. Bulk mechanical properties of water hyacinth. Journal of Aquatic Plant Mgt. 18:23-26

Bagnall, L.O.1981. Aquatic plant harvesting and harvesters. ASAE paper No.81-5019

Bagnall, L.L.1982. Bulk mechanical properties of Hydrilla. Journal of Aquatic Plant Management 20:49-53

Bernaki, H., Haman, J. And Kanafojski, Cz. 1972. Agricultural machines, theory and construction, Vol. 1 Published by the Scientific Publications Foreign Corporation Center of the Central Institute. Warsaw, Poland.

Calilung, E.J.1990. A system for rapid mechanical dewatering of water hyacinth. Unpublished Ph.D. Thesis. No. AE-90-5, Asian Institute of Technology, Bangkok, Thailand

Chancellor, W.J. 1955. Cutting of biological materials. CRC Handbook of Engineering in Agriculture, Volume I Crop Production Engineering, CRC Press, Inc. Florida.

pp. 39-63

Chancellor, W.J.1958. Energy requirements for cutting forage. Agricultural Engineering. 39 (10, 663

Chancellor, W.J. 1964. Balancing aids mechanical dewatering of forage. Trans. Of the ASAE 7 (4): 388-390.

Cifuentes, J. And L.O.Bagnall. 1976. Pressing characteristics of water hyacinth. Journal of Aquatic Plant Mgt. 14:71-75

Ferrero A: Horabik J.Molenda M 1991. Density-pressure relationship compaction of straw Canadian Agricultural Engineering, 33 (1) 107-111

Ferrero, A., J.Horabik and M.Molenda. 1992. Density-pressure relationship in compaction of straw. 1990. Canadian Agricultural Engineering pp 107-111

Gopal B.1983. Utilization of water hyacinth as a new resource for its control: some environmental considerations. Water hyacinth: proceedings on the international conference on water hyacinth. Hyderabad, India.

Gopal B. And K.P.Sharma. 1981. Water hyacinth. Hindustan Publishers D-35, C.C.Colony Delhi, India.

Kanafoski, C.Z. and T. Karwowski, 1976. Agricultural Machines: Theory and Construction Vol.2.

Lindsey, K. And H.M.Hirt, 1999. Use water hyacinth! A practical handbook of uses for the water hyacinth from across the World. Published by Drukerei Bauer, Winnenden, Germany.

Manual of Patent Practice and Procedure, Intellectual Property Office, India, Available at http://ipindia.nic.in/ipr/patent/DraftPatent_Manual_2008.pdf

Mathur S.M.2000. Study on volume and weight reduction of water hyacinth. Unpublished Ph.D.Thesis, Deptt. Of FM & PE, CTAE, Udaipur, India

Mathur, S.M., and P.Singh. 2002. Compression characteristics of chopped water hyacinth Indian Journal of Agricultural Sciences 72 (10): 619-21.

Mathur, S.M. and Pratap Singh 2004a. Development and performance evaluation of water hyacinth chopper cum crusher, International Journal of Bio system Engineering, U.K., 88(4) 411-418.

O'dogherty, M.J.1982. A review of research on forage chopping. Journal of Agric. Engng. Res., 27, 267-289.

Spencer, R.R., E, M, Bickoff, G.O.Kohler, S.C. Witt, Knuckles and A.Mottala. 1969. Alfalfa Product by wet fractionation. Trans. Of the ASAE. 13 (2): 198-200.

Steward III, John, 1972. Energy and flow requirement for chopping water hyacinth. Unpublished M.E.Thesis, University of Florida.

16

Appendices

Vimal KUmar Varun

Aooebdix A

Patent Offices

American Patent & Trademark Law Centre
http://www.patentpending.com
Australian Patent Office (IP Australia)
http://www.ipaustralia.gov.au
Austrian Patent Office
http://www.patentamt.at
Bangladesh-Department of Patents, Designs and Trademark
http://www.dpdt.gov.bd
Belgian Patent Office
http://economie.fgov.be.fr/entreprises/propriete_intellectuelle/
Brazilian Institute of Intellectual Property
http://www.inpi.gov.br
Canadian Intellectual Property Office
http://www.cipo.gc.ca
Croatian State Intellectual Patent Office
http://www.dziv.ht/en
Czech Industrial Property Office
http://www.upv.cz/en.html
Danish Patent and Trademark Office
http://www.dkpto.org
European Patent Office
http://www.epo.org

Finland National Board of Patent s and Registration
http://www.prh.fi/en.html
France- National Institute of Industrial Property
http://www.inpi.fr
Georgian National Intellectual Property Center
http://www.sak.patenti.org.ge
German Patent and Trademark Office
http://www.dpma.de/english/index.html
Greek Industrial Property Organization
http://www.obi.gr
Hong Kong Intellectual Property Department
http://www/ipd.gov.hk/eng/home.htm
Hungarian Intellectual Property Office
http://www.hpo.gov.in
Indonesia Patent Directorate
http:www.dgip.gov.id
Italian Patent and Trademark Office
http://www.uibm.gov.it
Japanese Patent Office
http://www.kipo.go.kr
Luxembourg Patent Office
http://www.eco.public.lu
Malaysia Intellectual Property Corporation
http://www.myipo.gov.my
Maracas Patent Office
http://www.oepm.es
Netherlands Patent Office
http://www.agentschapnl.nl/en/node/108069
New Zealand Intellectual Property Office
http://www.iponz.govt.nz
Pakistan Intellectual Property Organization
http://www.ipo.gov.pk
People's Republic of China state Intellectual Property Office
http://english.sipo.gov.cn
Polish Patent Office
http://www.uprp.pl
Portuguese Institute of Industry Property
http:/www. Marcasepatentes.pt
Singapore Intellectual Property Office
http://www.ipos.gov.sg
Slovenian Intellectual Property Office
http://www.uil-sipo-si
Sri Lanka National Intellectual Property Office
http://www.nipo.gov.lk
Swedish Patent and Registration Office
http://www.prv.se
Swiss Federal Institute of Intellectual Property
http://www.ige.ch/en.html

United Kingdom Intellectual Property Office
http://ww.ip.gov.uk
United States Patent and Trademark Office
http://www.uspto.gov
World Intellectual Property Organization (WIPO)
http://www.wipo.int
WIPO-PCT
http://www.wipo.int/pct/en/

Appendix – B

Organizations Supporting Innovations for Transformation of an Idea to Prototype to Pilot Plant to Commercialization

Centre for Innovation, Incubation and Entrepreneurship (CIIE), Ahmedaba,d India
http://www.ciieindia.org

Council of Scientific and Industrial Research, New Delhi, India
http://www.csir.res.in

Department of Science and Technology, New Delhi, India
http://www.dst.gov.in

Department of Scientific and Industrial Research (DSIR), New Delhi, India
http://www.dsir.gov.in

Grassroots Innovation Augmentation network (GIAN), Ahmedabad, India
http://www.gian.org

National Innovation Foundation (NIF), Ahmedabad, India
http.ww.nifindia.org

Science and Technology Entrepreneurship Park (STEP), New Delhi, India
http://www.nstedb.com/institutional /step.htm

Society for research and Initiatives for Sustainable Technologies and Institutions (SRISTI), Ahmedabad, India
http://www.sristi.org

Technology Business Incubators (TBIs), New Delhi, India
http://www.nstedb.com/institutional/tbi.htm

Technology Development Board (TDB), New Delhi, India
http.ww.tdb.gov.in

Technology Information, Forecasting and Assessment Council (TIFAC), New Delhi, India
http://www.tifac.org.in

Appendix – C

Organizations promoting, facilitating, Technology Development, Transfer, Utilization, commercialization

Confederation of Indian Industries (CII), New Delhi, India
http://www.cii.in

Consultancy Development centre (CDC), New Delhi India
http://www.cdc.org.in

Council of Scientific and Industrial Research (CSIR), New Delhi, India
http://www.csir.org.in

Department of Biotechnology (DBT), New Delhi, India
http://www.dbindia.gov.in

Department of Electronics and Information Technology (DeitY), New Delhi, India
http://www.deity.gov.in

Department of Science and Technology (DST), New Delhi, India
http://www.dst.gov.in

Department of Scientific and Industrial Research (DSIR), New Delhi, India
http://www.dsir.gov.in

Federation of Indian Chambers of Commerce and Industry (FICCI), New Delhi, India
http:/www.ficci.com

Foundation for Innovation and Technology Transfer (FITT), New Delhi, India
http:.//www.fitt.iitd.org

Indian Trade Promotion Organization (ITPO), New Delhi, India
http://www.indiatradefair.org

Indian Institute of Foreign Trade (IIFT), Centre for International Trade in Technology (CITT), New Delhi, India
http://www.cc.iift.ac.in/docs/iift/citt.asp

Ministry of Micro, Small and Medium Enterprises (MSME), New Delhi, India
http://www.msme.gov.in

National Research Development Organization (NRDC), India
http://www.nrdcindia.com

National Science & Technology Entrepreneurship Development Board (NSTEDB), DST, New Delhi, INDIA
http://www.nstedb.com

Society for Research and Initiatives for Sustainable Technologies and Institutions (SRISTI), Ahmedabad, India
http://www.sristi.org

Technology Trade Facilitation Centre (TTFC), National Research development Corporation (NRDC), New Delhi, INDIA

http:/www.nrdcindia.com/ttfct.htm

Technology Innovation Management and Entrepreneurship Information Service (TIMEIS), NSTEDB, INDIA

http://www.techno-preneur.net

Technology Information, Forecasting and Assessment Council (TIFAC), New Delhi, India

http://www.tifac.org.in

Appendix – D

Patent Softwares

USPTO EFS-Web

http://www.uspto.gov/patents/process/file/efs/

EFS-Web is the United States patent and Trademark Office's (USPTO's) Web-based patent application and document submission solution. Using EFS-Web, anyone with a Web-enabled computer can file patent applications and documents without downloading special software or changing document preparation tools and processes.

EFS-Web utilizes standard Web-based screens and prompts to enable you to submit patent application documents in PDF format directly to the USPTO within minutes. When creating your PDF documents, you choose the tool, process and workflow with which you author your documents, convert them to standard PDF files and then submit them to USPTO's secure servers. Additionally, EFS-Web allows submission of PCT-EASY. ZIP compressed files to submit International PCT applications and ASCII text files (.TXT) TO submit your bio-sequence listing, computer program listing, mega tables, etc. EFS-Web is safe, simple and secure and gives you all of the same benefits as paper filings, including an electronic receipt that acknowledges your submission date.

Patent Wizard (US Provisional Patent Application Software)

http:/www.patentwizard.com

Created by Michael S Neustel, Registered Patent Attorney (http://www.patent.ideas.com) in the year 2000. Two versions are available as Patent Wizard Professional and Patent Wizard online.

EPO Online Services

http://www.epo.org/applying/online-servies.html

EPO Online services have been designed to allow applicants, attorneys and other users to conduct their EPO business electronically in a secure state-of-the-art environment. This includes Online filing and Online fee payment.

Online filing software is used to file EP, Euro-PCT and PCT applications; submissions in opposition, appeal, limitation and revocation proceedings before the EPO; and subsequently filed documents for all EP proceeding. One can also use it to file applications and documents with participating national offices.

The detail for online filing is available at http://www.epo.org/applying/online-services/online-filing.html.

WIPO PCT-SAFE Software

http://www.wipo.int/pct.safe/en/

The software offers PCT users the means to prepare their international applications in electronic form and to file them online, on physical media or in PCT-EASY mode. FAQ on PCT-SAFE is available at http://www.wipo.int/pct-safe/en/faq.html. PCT-SAFE Client version (3.51.059.235) dated April 1,2013 is available for download at http://www.wipo.int/pct-afe/en/download/download-client.html along with the instructions for installation

Patent Pro (Thinking outside the Box)

http://www.4patpro.com

Patent Pro creates the patent application using its own patented process. It even helps you write the claims like a seasoned patent attorney with patented Add-A-Claim Feature and Guides through the patent process automatically. It generates all the forms and helps to prepare drawings. It contains all the materials needed to file the complete patent application with the United States Patent and Trademark Office.

Kolibri 360 GmbH
Ferdinand-Jühlke-Straße 7
99095 Erfurt, Deutschland
produktsicherheit@kolibri360.de